# FOLLOWING ORDERS

# ORDERS

## The Death of Vince Foster, Clinton White House Lawyer

ONE ROCK INK PUBLISHING

## MARINKA PESCHMANN

MARINKA PESCHMANN

*A sequel to:*

# THE
# WHISTLEBLOWER

**How the Clinton White House Stayed in
Power to Reemerge in the Obama White
House and the World Stage**

## *Following Orders*

First Edition
ISBN: 978-0-9878343-2-4
Library of Congress information available
Scripture quotations marked (ESV) are from The Holy Bible, English Standard Version® (ESV®), Copyright © 2001 by Crossway, a publishing ministry of Good News Publishers. Used by permission. All rights reserved. Scripture quotations noted as (NIV) are taken from THE HOLY BIBLE, NEW INT-ERNATIONAL VERSION® (NIV®), Copyright © 1973, 1978, 1984, 2011 by Biblica, Inc.™ Used by permission. All rights reserved worldwide. Scripture verses noted as (NKJV) are taken from the New King James Version. Copyright © 1982 by Thomas Nelson, Inc. Used by permission. All rights reserved. All Bible scriptures may be found at: biblegateway.com.
Published by One Rock Ink Publishing
Canada
Printed in the United States

"Take no part in the unfruitful works of darkness, but instead expose them."  —Ephesians 5:11 (ESV)

# Dedication

To truth-tellers who stand tall in the face of adversity and deception, who have the courage to speak truth to power—and never cave in to evil.

# CONTENTS

# Cast of Characters

## KEY PLAYERS

**Hillary Rodham Clinton,** former first lady of the United States (1993-2001)

**William Jefferson Clinton,** former president of the United States

**Vincent Foster,** deputy counsel to the President of the United States William Jefferson Clinton, Bill Clinton's childhood friend, and Hillary Clinton's closest Rose Law Firm colleague, trusted confidante

**Bernard (Bernie) Nussbaum,** chief counsel to the president, shared a long history with Hillary that went back to President Richard Nixon's Watergate impeachment effort, resigned humiliated in disgrace over his mishandling of the Whitewater and Foster investigations

**Linda Tripp,** Bernard Nussbaum's executive assistant in the White House presidential counsel's office, ex-army wife and career civil servant, who in 1998 made international headlines after she began taping Monica Lewinsky, President Clinton's paramour, for insurance to protect herself from the Clintons as they attempted to fix *another* court case at which she would be called to testify

## WHITE HOUSE AND ADMINISTRATION STAFFERS

**Betsy Pond,** Bernard Nussbaum's secretary

**Deborah Gorham,** Vince Foster's personal executive assistant

**Tom Castletown,** White House intern

**Bruce Lindsey,** deputy counsel to the president, longtime Arkansas friend and Little Rock attorney

**Steve Neuwirth,** associate White House counsel, brought to Washington from Bernie Nussbaum's New York law firm

1

**Craig Livingston,** director of White House security, an ex-bouncer from Arkansas, who took the fall for improperly obtaining hundreds of Federal Bureau of Investigations security clearances of Republicans that illegally ended up in the West Wing during the Clinton Filegate investigation; resigned disgraced

**William Kennedy,** counsel to the president, longtime Arkansas friend, Rose Law Firm lawyer, who was reprimanded in the Clinton Travelgate investigation

**Maggie Williams,** Hillary's chief of staff and longtime friend from Arkansas, who accepted $50,000 during the Clintons' campaign finance scandal investigation, "Chinagate"

**Patsy Thomasson,** director of White House administration, with access to the West Wing despite not having a security clearance, also involved in the travel office investigation, long-time Arkansas ties

**David Watkins,** White House operation director, also involved in Travelgate, and longtime Arkansas friend

**Dee Dee Myers,** press secretary

**George Stephanopoulos,** Clinton communications director

**Mark Gearan,** White House chief of communications director

**Thomas Franklin "Mack" McLarty,** chief of staff, a lifelong friend of Bill Clinton and Vince Foster from Arkansas

**Webster Hubbell,** top Justice Department official, longtime Clinton friend, Hillary's close colleague at Arkansas' Rose Law firm, indicted three times and convicted in the Whitewater investigations

**Deb Coyle,** worked outside President Bill Clinton's Oval office

**Henry P. O'Neill,** secret service officer, an eighteen-year veteran

## OFFICE OF INDEPENDENT COUNSEL (OIC)
**Robert Fiske,** independent counsel
**Kenneth Starr,** independent counsel


## U.S. PARK POLICE INVESTIGATORS
**Chief Robert Langston**
**Major Robert Hines**
**Detective Peter Markland**
**John Rolla**
**Cheryl Braun**


**CW,** Confidential Witness
**Lisa Foster,** Vince Foster's wife

# Prologue

**W**hile it might have initially appeared that the deputy counsel to the president of the United States was taking a nap in a park—lying neatly face-up on a steep embankment with his feet pointing down—Vincent W. Foster Jr. was not napping. He was dead. Dressed in expensive trousers and a white dress shirt, less than eight miles from the White House, he was lying dead. A single gunshot wound to the head. Dead. Some of the blood on Foster's face was still wet, but starting to dry. A trail of blood *flowed upwards* from his nose to above his ear.[1] The man who found his body said there was no gun, but after he left to notify police, a gun appeared in Foster's hand.[2] It was July 20, 1993. President William Jefferson Clinton's Arkansas childhood friend, and First Lady Hillary Clinton's Rose Law Firm partner, and White House confidante was dead.

At the pinnacle of his law career, where rumors of a U.S. Supreme Court appointment abounded, Foster, the loving husband and father of three, who worked directly with the most powerful couple in the world, was dead.[3] The tall, handsome, Southern gentleman, would never see his forty-ninth birthday, never laugh, smile, or speak again. The twinkle in his hazel eyes was forever darkened. Vince Foster was dead.

It was an executive assistant in Hillary's presidential counsel's office, Linda Tripp, who was officially one of the last people to have seen Foster alive in the White House.

White House reporter: "Considering Mr. Foster's position and his status [in the Clinton White House], isn't it reasonable to assume that law enforcement agencies are at least going to make some attempt to determine a motive here? For example, if you don't do that, you'll leave open wild possibilities, such as that he may have been being blackmailed or anything like that—just to rule those things out? Don't you think it's reasonable that a law enforcement agency will attempt to establish a motive?"

Clinton Press Secretary Dee Dee Myers: "My only point, is that at this point, the Park Service Police is the only agency that's investigating [Vince Foster's death], and that the objective of their search is simply to determine that it was a suicide."[4]

Are we clear? The objective of the investigation into Vince Foster's death was "simply *to determine that it was a suicide* [emphasis mine]." The conclusion was predetermined. From the get-go, homicide, foul play, the possibility of blackmail, a potential risk to America's national security, was never investigated. Facts be damned. Vince Foster committed suicide in Fort Marcy Park. No need for the Clinton White House to cooperate with investigators or the press. They didn't. Case closed. Move on …

In America there has been a slow, creeping destruction of the freedom of speech and of the rule of law, and soon all Americans will lose free speech completely if they do not fight for it now. Though the road to silencing legitimate questions from the media and Americans alike may have been a long, deliberate one, crafted by those in power like Hillary and Bill Clinton—used to stay in power, and to thwart the rule of law—it becomes harder to reverse the silencing trend, expose government malfeasance, and hold corruption accountable if people do not stand up and speak now. Like an undiagnosed cancer, silence permits corruption to grow. Not to speak is to speak. You *must* choose your side.

The word "cover-up" is defined as: "a usually concerted effort to keep an illegal or unethical act or situation from being made public."[5]

It has often been said in the history of modern political scandals, that the cover-up is much worse than the crime or the incident. I will leave that to you to decide.

The First Amendment to the United States Constitution states: "Congress shall make no law ... abridging the freedom of speech, or of the press ...." Despite the fact that Vince Foster's sudden death was the shocking and questionable passing of the highest ranking U.S. government official since President John Kennedy was assassinated on November 22, 1963, asking obvious questions about it became taboo and politically incorrect.

Even though the Senate Whitewater Committee investigation's conclusion revealed that there was "a concerted effort by senior White House officials to block career law enforcement investigators from conducting a thorough investigation" into Foster's death, and recommended "that steps be taken to insure that such misuse of the White House counsel's office does not recur in this, or any future, administration," meaningful and honest reporting was still attacked.[6] Journalists or investigators who dared to speak truth to power by asking legitimate and common-sense questions were sidelined, mocked, dismissed as right-wing hacks or scolded by Hillary for inflicting "great emotional and monetary damage on innocent people." [7]

Americans no longer had a right to know what was happening in their White House, and the lawlessness and secrecy in government has only gotten worse ever since. This is one of the many reasons why the Foster story must be told now. As history is repeating itself in the scandal-ridden Obama-Clinton regime—from Fast and Furious, to Wikileaks and Benghazi-Gate—investigators are being thwarted once again, and Americans are in danger around the world and at home.[8]

Yet despite that, the Obama-Clinton regime was reelected to lead America for a second term. Hillary and Bill Clinton are being re-crafted as moderates, and speculation for a Hillary 2016 presidential run endures whether or not she remains serving as President Obama's Secretary of State. It's upside down. Americans deserve to know what happened in their White House and they have been lied to. Americans deserve to know what is happening in their White House now and always and they are still being lied to with no accountability or consequence in sight.

This must end—now.

As President John F. Kennedy said during a speech in New York entitled, "The President and the Press," on April 27, 1961, "The very word 'secrecy' is repugnant in a free and open society; and we are as a people inherently and historically opposed to secret societies, to secret oaths and to secret proceedings. We decided long ago that the dangers of excessive and unwarranted concealment of pertinent facts far outweighed the dangers which are cited to justify it … Without debate, without criticism, no administration, and no country can succeed, and no republic can survive."[9]

———

When the tape recordings of a career civil servant, Linda Tripp, an ex-Army wife and single mother, with Monica Lewinsky became public in January 1998, President Bill Clinton's affair with a subordinate government intern/employee was exposed. His attempted cover-up to fix a court case, and obstruct justice (not the Clintons' first attempt) was also brought to light and the revelations led to only the second president in American history to face impeachment.

Although what Tripp, (the last person to have "officially" seen Foster alive in the White House), had recorded was accurate, and it was President Clinton who had lied to Americans, to keep themselves in power, Hillary ignited a vicious politics of personal destruction campaign against her by accusing a false "vast right-wing conspiracy" of attempting to destroy her supposedly innocent husband. The intimidating fallout against Tripp included the illegal leaking of her confidential FBI files (the case was ultimately settled in Tripp's favor) and a trumped-up criminal prosecution (eventually the case was dismissed).[10] Indeed the justice system—in an attempt to criminalize innocent Americans into silence—was used for political gain.

The Clintons' political survival depended on their "ends justify the means" Saul Alinsky progressive philosophy where they (and other politicians like President Barack Obama) will do *anything* to stay in power.

These Alinskyite tactics were not exclusive to the Clinton-Lewinsky scandal but as I reported in *The Whistleblower: How the Clinton White House Stayed in Power to Reemerge in the Obama White House and on the World Stage,* they occurred during all the Clinton investigations, including the Foster death investigations, and are being used again to thwart the Obama-Clinton regime investigations.

The "ends justify the means" tactics are those of Saul Alinsky, the father of community organizing and author of *Rules for Radicals*—the guidebook to pushing a progressive, social justice way of life onto America at any cost. In Alinsky's view and that of his acolytes, progressive social justice is the redistribution of wealth and the primacy of the societal good over individual liberty. His teachings are the blueprint for progressives, most notably Hillary Clinton and Barack Obama.[11] Alinsky's book, dedicated to "the first radical known to man who rebelled against the establishment and did it so effectively that he at least won his own kingdom—Lucifer," became the inspiration for several leftist politicians and undeniably extended their political life spans.[12]

Contrary to the media portrayal and public misperception, the vilification of Linda Tripp did not transpire because of Bill Clinton's sexual escapades in the Oval office; rather, the ugly truth is found in what happened during the *earlier* investigations when Tripp served in Bill Clinton's Oval office and Hillary Clinton's presidential counsel office *with Vince Foster*. That truth would have otherwise landed everyday Americans in contempt of court, charged with obstruction of justice, or in prison.

For the first time you will know why Linda Tripp tape recorded Monica Lewinsky for an insurance policy to protect herself from the Clintons—and from a perjury charge if she told the truth under oath when President Clinton (once more making a mockery of the rule of law) lied under oath ... again.

Now, in *Following Orders: The Death of Vince Foster, Clinton White House Lawyer,* I finish what I began in *The Whistleblower,* and report the full story of the Vince Foster death investigations. As you will see, the official findings, forced to draw their conclusions using the "available evidence" were wrong. Instead, based on the new information I obtained from Linda Tripp—*who had been a Clinton "team-player,"* and evidence from the official investigations, you are led to a terrible conclusion and to a massive cover-up: Vince Foster did not commit suicide in Fort Marcy Park, Virginia—he died in his White House office.

No longer will Americans wonder how Washington became so broken when they see how those in power thwart the rule of law, obstruct justice, corrupt formerly principled, God-fearing people, and are never held to account thanks to the failure of both the Republican and Democrat leadership—even at the deadly expense of long-time loyal friends and colleagues.

The following pages are the work of a true crime investigation in a story that may read like fiction, but it is not. This is what happened in your White House. Come, join me and dare to speak truth to power.

— Marinka Peschmann

# 1
# It Does Not Take a Village

"Jesus answered them, 'Most assuredly,
I say to you, whoever commits sin is a slave of sin.'"

**—John 8:34 (NKJV)**

The air was still in Middleburg, Virginia. The only sounds came from the crickets outside.

"Linda, let's go back to the day Vince Foster died," I said.

There we were, Linda Tripp and I, in the summer of 2000, secluded in a private, gated estate on a horse farm in a guesthouse above a four-car garage, across from the magnificent main house. It was the temporary apartment Linda had rented to escape her Maryland home, because her address had been printed in the newspapers during the events that led to U.S. President William Jefferson Clinton's impeachment.

Tripp, a single mom and career civil servant had served outside President Bill Clinton's Oval office and inside First Lady Hillary Rodham Clinton's presidential counsel's office. She had been subpoenaed to testify in the Clinton White House investigations from Travelgate to Whitewater—and the Foster death investigation.

A little history here is necessary. In 1998, Tripp made international headlines when her secretly taped conversations with a former White House intern, Monica Lewinsky, became public. Lewinsky disclosed on those recordings that she had been sexually involved with President Clinton in the White House. Clinton had denied the affair and was accused of suborning perjury, obstruction of justice, and witness tampering to cover it up in an attempt to fix a sexual harassment court case. Hillary had defended her guilty husband and branded his accusers, including Linda Tripp, as part of "a vast right-wing conspiracy" bent on destroying the president.[13] As the political war escalated in the media, however, a problem emerged: the "vast right-wing conspiracy" was right. The president had been sexually involved with Monica Lewinsky. Tripp's recordings were accurate. He had lied under oath, and Linda did not want to lie under oath in the Paula Jones sexual harassment case against the president.[14]

While Linda had testified that she had made those tape recordings as an insurance policy to protect herself from the Clintons—and from being caught in a false perjury charge if *she* told the truth under oath and President Clinton lied (he did)—the media following the Clinton White House narrative didn't buy it.[15] Tripp was an evil, gossipy villain, a rabid Republican bent on destroying them, they declared while endlessly vilifying her. But the media elite were wrong. Linda was a registered Independent who—she had admitted to me and testified under oath—had actually been a Clinton team player.[16]

"With all the different investigations I felt like I had been a team player," she even admitted to the mainstream press, a critical detail they chose to ignore. "It bothered my sense of values—it did—it bothered me, but I was selfish. I wanted my job," Linda said. "I wanted my livelihood. So for security I shut up." This was the excuse she fell back on when attempting to justify her crisis of conscience and decision to testify exactly as the Clinton White House had instructed her and all of the staffers.[17]

Indeed, as reported in *The Whistleblower,* Linda had protected the Clintons in all the earlier investigations—

which is the real reason she needed to be discredited and destroyed during the events that led to only the second president in the history of the United States being impeached. It had nothing to do with sex.

And now, as Hillary was making history running for the junior New York State Senate seat, a stepping stone for her planned presidential run (which came to pass, and failed in 2007, and may happen again in the 2016 presidential contest), the criminal wiretapping charges that had been filed against Linda for taping her conversations with Monica Lewinsky had been dropped.[18] Linda was finally free to set the record straight on the Clinton era where she had served—or so I had thought.

With Cleo, Linda's golden retriever dog, gently asleep at her usual spot, in front of the living room couch, I faced the computer and clicked print. Page after page rolled out documenting the events of July 20, 1993—that was the day White House deputy counsel to the president of the United States, Vincent Walker Foster Jr., was found dead of an apparent self-inflicted gunshot wound to the head in Fort Marcy Park in McLean, Virginia. It was the highest-ranking suicide in government since 1949, when President Truman's secretary of defense, James Forrestal, committed suicide by throwing himself from a sixteenth floor window to his death from the Bethesda Naval Hospital.[19]

Foster was the son of a real-estate broker, who excelled at virtually everything he did, from athletics to academics. The former student-body president at Hope High School, in 1967 Foster graduated from Davidson College. During his first year of law school, at Vanderbilt, he married Elizabeth "Lisa" Braden at St. Henry Catholic Church in Nashville in April 1968. As Lisa later recounted in an interview in *The New Yorker* she had "kissed him on the first date"—something she had never done in her life. Having fallen head over heels in love with him, "Vince seemed so smart and so interested in the world."[20] The happy couple would go on to have three children.

In 1971 Foster transferred to the University of Arkansas law school in Fayetteville, where he earned the top score on the state's bar examination. Two years after joining the powerful Little Rock, Arkansas, Rose Law Firm he was made partner. It was Foster along with Rose Law Firm partner Webster Hubbell, "a big burly, likable man ... who was a great fun to work with and loyal supportive friend," as described by Hillary, who were among a handful of Arkansans who went to Washington to serve in the Clinton administration;[21] Foster in Hillary's presidential counsel's office, and Hubbell, as associate attorney general, in the Justice department. In fact, Foster was instrumental in hiring Hillary as the first female associate at the Rose Law Firm. Admittedly, Hillary worked most closely with both Foster and Hubbell, with Foster for nearly fifteen years.[22] Bill Clinton was governor of Arkansas at the time.

"Vince Foster's backyard touched [Bill Clinton's] when he lived with his grandparents in Hope, Arkansas. [Bill and Vince] were friends virtually all their lives ...[23] "Foster was one of the best lawyers [Hillary] had ever known and one of the best friends" she had ever had ... "steady, courtly, sharp but understated, the sort of person you would want around in times of trouble."[24]

Linda, officially one of the last people to have seen Vince Foster alive in Hillary's White House counsel's office, served as executive assistant to the chief counsel to the president, Bernard "Bernie" Nussbaum. For her, the sudden death of Bill and Hillary's long-time friend and confidante was her first encounter with the idea of suicide. The haunting "Why? Why? Why?" questions that could never be answered taunted her. "Why did Vince do it? What was so terrible?" she would say to me, giving her troubled thoughts a voice. "Why didn't I see something and stop him, help him?" she cried out at times, still blaming herself.

After Foster, the tall, handsome, elegant, Southern gentleman died, it was easy for Linda to immerse herself at work, and shove aside the maddening guilt and disturbing thoughts that she had somehow failed him; but at night the haunting reflections crept back in. Her mind repeated. *Could I have stopped him?*

In search of peace, answers, anything, she drove to the nearest bookstore, bought everything that dealt with death and suicide, and, like former Clinton communications aide George Stephanopoulos, Linda sought outside help. Stephanopoulos began weekly sessions with a therapist "for all the usual reasons," but the reasons "were magnified by the shock of Foster's suicide."[25] For Linda, no book, no person could explain, nor did the official findings appear to calm her angst. Linda's angst manifested itself in a form you could see: her weight gain that began after Foster died.

When I met Linda in 2000, seven years had passed since his death; and her self-recriminations had not faded. Foster's death seemed to eat at her soul, sometimes over-whelming her when I brought it up. Instead of answering my questions—questions prompted by her testimony and public statements, she fueled my curiosity by changing the subject to safer territory; to another gossipy Monica Lewinsky story perhaps. Other times she exclaimed, "I don't know what really happened," or she hid behind her self-constructed wall of rationalizations. "Casting blame won't bring Vince back," she'd insist, "nor is it my place to lay credence to conspiracy theories." Which was true—if the official findings were correct.

It was Linda who suggested otherwise when she testified during Special Prosecutor Kenneth Starr's Office of Independent Counsel Clinton-Lewinsky grand jury: "I had reason to believe that the Vince Foster tragedy was not depicted accurately under oath by members of the administration ... and these are, remember, instances of national significance that included testimony by, also, Mrs. Clinton, also in Travelgate. It became very important for them for their version of events to be the accepted version of events," she testified. "I knew based on my personal knowledge, personal observations that they were lying under oath. So it became very fearful for me that I had information even back then that was very dangerous."[26]

But what also really heightened my suspicions about the circumstances surrounding his death was that we had gone over the Clintons' stay-in-power tactics, such as the "cohesive strategy" tactic: a smoke and mirrors public relations trick where the White House would tell Americans and investigators what they wanted them to know as opposed to what really happened, and how their scripted version would became the so-called truth, the 'talking points,' the narrative picked up by the press—regardless of any inconvenient facts that would pop up. I knew how those tactics worked.[27] So why did Linda constantly contradict herself?

"No one challenged Hillary, not low-on-the-totem-pole me all the way up to senior staff and the president," Linda repeatedly said, clearly still intimidated.

Yet, after all this time, she still heeded their warnings. "What couldn't you tell investigators about Vince's death then that you wanted them to know but were too afraid to tell?" I'd ask her.

And she would dodge, sometimes getting angry. "I

told you," she bristled, "I was afraid I'd lose my job. I had kids at home, my pension. You don't understand. You don't have kids."

And she was right; but at the same time, I could not help but wonder what she could lose now—if there was something to tell. She had been trashed by the media on a global scale during the events that led to President Bill Clinton's impeachment, was threatened, put into a safe house by agents from the Federal Bureau of Investigations (FBI) and the Office of Independent Counsel (OIC), felt the full force of the Clinton machine, and as a political appointee serving in the Clinton administration, like all political appointees, was about to lose her job after the 2000 elections when the George W. Bush administration would take office.[28] Her kids, now young adults, Alison and Ryan, had left home; and still all these years later, she remained tight-lipped and defensive. How could I not think she was hiding something? But what was it?

One afternoon, out of the blue, Linda surprisingly and unnecessarily apologized for her grief over Foster's death. She was afraid it might appear disproportionate, considering the short time she had known him (which was not quite six months). She wanted to be clear.

"Vince was not just someone I worked for, but a friend," she said defending her sorrow. Then she over-compensated by describing how their bond was forged quickly with a shared camaraderie amid their hectic high-pressure jobs in Hillary's counsel's office. Other times she would simply lament, "If only Vince were alive ..." how "Vince would've understood" —referring to her predicament with the Clintons.

"You could trust Vince with anything, such a decent soul," she told me. "I wish you could've met him."

Often she would share endearing anecdotes about

how much Foster loved and adored his family. He surrounded himself with photos of them in his office. Or she would reminisce how he would chisel out time during his demanding White House schedule to lift someone else up whenever he could. Sometimes he would stop her on her way out the door of the counsel's office, and ask if she would mind dropping off an envelope for him to mail, only to see it was a letter of encouragement addressed to a young student in Little Rock who had expressed an interest in law school.

In the cramped suite in the West Wing's counsel's office Linda could overhear Vince on the Dictaphone dictating letter after letter full of kind words and encouraging advice to young Americans, "When I first started out ... Go for it, it's your dream," even sometimes typing the letters up for him. "That was Vince, always taking the time to lift another person up," she would sadly reminisce.

Ironically, had he lived, Foster would have been the person she would have trusted to help her navigate through the treacherous months of President Clinton's impeachment.

"You know people just don't know," Linda would warn me. "Vince wasn't like them," referring to the Clintons. "He wasn't ruthless. Hillary is ruthless. Vince cared about people. He was genuine—they're not. Only when the camera is running do they act like they care."

For the Clintons, who had also suffered a loss, Foster's death sparked a firestorm that engulfed the nation. The charges leveled against them were serious: Foster knew too much. *They had killed him.* Clinton staffers removed files from his office. *Must be a cover-up.* Investigators never found the fatal bullet. *It's a conspiracy.* And on and on it went.

Despite five government investigations that concluded Foster committed suicide in Fort Marcy Park, the conspiracy beast was still on the prowl. With my reporter's cap fastened tightly on, I was ready to find out the truth. Were the Foster conspiracy theories viable or were they created by the Right for political gain?

Having finished dinner, Linda emerged from the kitchen and sat on the couch across from me. Ahead would be a long night. I spun my chair around to face her. Steadying my feet on the table rim, I lightly brushed against two large three-ringed black binders. Inside the binders housed what the public knew: copies of White House press briefings and investigative reports into Vince Foster's death, including the Office of Independent Counsel (OIC) Reports with media articles stacked along-side them. Handing Linda a copy of what I had reconstructed using public records interwoven with fragmented details she had cautiously shared over six months, I glanced at her, trying to gauge her mood. Would she procrastinate, balk, or change the subject as before? Or would she explain what she meant: why the White House dishonesty during the Foster investigations had shaken her so? [29]

That night would be my chance to find out.

Could we vindicate the innocent? Expose the guilty if guilt applied? Bring closure and peace to Foster's family? Clear the cloud of suspicion hovering over Bill and Hillary? Was even thinking we could end the controversy a farfetched hope? Frankly, I wondered if anyone could, but I had to try.

Unbeknownst to me, I was about to learn something Linda had kept hidden about Foster's death that challenged her conscience and eventually defeated it. And I would see how great a burden it had been, how it defined the person she became, governed the future choices she had made—and revealed the motivation behind wanting "insurance" to protect herself from the Clintons when she taped Monica Lewinsky to avoid being set up in a perjury trap during the Paula Jones sexual harassment case against President Bill Clinton. [30]

Because what I learned challenged the official findings in the Foster case. The reporter in me could not drop the implications of Linda's confession. Nor could I ignore it, forget about it, or look the other way. I prayed to the good Lord above for guidance, and I was compelled to go back and re-investigate, check, crosscheck, double check, and research to verify that what I had concluded was not just a hunch, not some conspiracy theory that could be debunked or the Clintons could dismiss and call fiction. I had an advantage others before me did not have. I had the evidence of years of official investigations, as well as what fellow journalists had reported, to draw upon.

The secret Linda kept about Vince Foster had tormented her—she permitted it to do so by continuing to keep it, and by covering for the Clintons to ensure their White House days would not be numbered and she would keep her job—or so she thought. But for me, knowing the secret became a blessing and a curse; a curse because of the tremendously tough, frustrating journey that unknowingly lay before me as I sat across from Linda that day. The secret turned back into a blessing, praise God, because uncovering the truth about Vince Foster's death vindicates the innocent, exposes guilt and a wicked cover-up at the hands of America's self-serving, and morally bankrupt leaders.

America deserves to know what happens inside their White House. Americans deserve honest elected (and un-elected) God-fearing leaders who respect and honor the rule of law (as opposed to leaders who *think and act* as if they are God and above the law). I hope by telling the story, now, I can bring long overdue peace to Foster's family, and provide a jarring wake-up call to both sides of the political aisle to stop playing politics at the expense of Americans and of the truth by ensuring that justice finally be served. No one in America—and that includes Hillary and Bill Clinton—is above the law.

It would not take a village to alter the outcome of Foster's death, just a handful of people. And remarkably, both sides of the aisle—were *half* right. All this time what may have happened to Foster has been in the middle and hiding in plain sight.

# 2

# The Last Day

"When I looked for good, then evil came unto me:
And when I waited for light, there came darkness."

**— Job 30:26 (KJV)**

It was July 20, 1993, less than an hour before the 9:00 a.m. scheduled nomination for Judge Louis Freeh as Federal Bureau of Investigations (FBI) Director.

The morning sun shone brightly, illuminating the White House. The Rose Garden air was fragrant with the scent of blossoming flowers. White folding chairs were clicked out and lined up in perfect rows facing the raised podium bearing the seal of the President of the United States. Smartly dressed White House stewards hurriedly and masterfully completed the finishing touches for the Rose Garden ceremony. In the background, the press corps was poised to cover the latest news.

Inside the Clinton White House counsel's office, the staffers came in early to race through last-minute preparations. As Linda recalled it, her boss, chief counsel to the president, Bernard "Bernie" Nussbaum, "was engaged in his office with Freeh, and a handful of his associates from New Jersey." An enormously organized, brass-knuckled, and well-respected New York City lawyer, Nussbaum shared a long history with Hillary that went back to President Richard Nixon's Watergate investigation where they led the effort to impeach him.[31] "Attorney General Janet Reno and Acting FBI Director Floyd Clark were conferring with Vice President Al Gore. Betsy [Betsy Pond: Nussbaum's secretary], Deb [Deborah Gorham: Foster's personal executive assistant since March 8, 1993], and I were bogged down with last minute details. Judge Freeh's nomination was so sudden we weren't given much notice to prepare the logistics," Linda stated.

Less than twenty-four hours earlier, President Clinton "hated to be the first president" ever to have to fire an FBI director, but he was when he fired Director Williams Sessions on "the recommendation" of his attorney general Janet Reno after Sessions "refused to resign despite numerous problems within the agency."[32]

Not everyone agreed. Director Sessions was at the helm during Travelgate, the first Clinton investigation where the White House fired long-serving travel office staffers, including Billy Dale, the travel office director. Dale was indicted under the false pretense of irregular accounting and eventually exonerated.[33] There were those (predominately on the Right) who saw his firing as a cover-up. The *Wall Street Journal* wrote, "The gang that pulled the great travel office caper is now hell-bent on firing the head of the FBI."[34]

(In January 1994, Sessions released a statement accusing the Clintons of politicizing the FBI, and hampering its ability to investigate Vince Foster's death.)[35]

It was just before nine o'clock when an impatient Steve Neuwirth, counsel to the president, called Linda from outside. He asked her to ask Nussbaum what he should do if the press brought up any of the investigations. Linda assumed he meant the travel office, and told him to say what they always did: "We don't comment on ongoing investigations." But Neuwirth apparently was not satisfied, "Look, Linda, I didn't call for your opinion. I want Bernie's."

Linda recalled that Nussbaum was with Freeh and she did not want to disturb them.

"So then Steve says to me, 'For f—k sake, Linda. Where's Vince?' I told him, he was alone in his office, and he insists I interrupt him."

"Did Steve always speak to you like that?" I asked her.

"It wasn't personal," she defended. "I think it had to do with the unbelievable pressures we faced. These Bill and Hillary investigations definitely got the best of us."

Reluctantly, Linda knocked on Foster's door trim to his small office with one window. Had it been any other day, Foster would have been in the meeting with Nussbaum and Freeh, but not this day, and that surprised her. That day, Foster was quietly skimming through papers alone when Linda relayed Steve's question. "Sorry to bother you, Vince," she said, "but Steve's on the phone and he wants to know how do we answer press inquiries to the investigations?" Foster looked up at her silently with a blank look. Linda thought he did not hear her, so she repeated herself, but she received another blank, vacant look.

It was unusual to ask him a question twice. "Vince was acting so out of character." Normally, he was the first one with a quick answer, usually answering questions before they were asked. Three times, Linda recalled asking him. "It was like he was a million miles away, so I asked if he was all right."

"You're sure Vince heard you?" I asked her.

"Yes, each time, I spoke louder, until he acknowledged me, but his tone was distant, he said, 'Oh, umm, what did you say?' So I repeated Steve's question, and asked for the okay. Finally, Vince answered. 'Yeah, okay. That's fine.' he said."

Judge Freeh's nomination started late. President Clinton's tardiness delayed it until 9:27 a.m. The counsel's office emptied out to the Rose Garden where Linda, Betsy, and Deb watched from the sidelines. Under the podium, senior White House lawyers, except for Foster, gathered with Judge Freeh's wife, their four sons, and the president. Linda's memory was sharp, I crosschecked it against other news accounts when she rattled off the attendees who sat among mainly law enforcement representatives and included Vice President Al Gore, Attorney General Janet Reno, acting FBI Director Clark, and New York U.S. Senator Alfonse D'Amato.[36] Hillary, who was out of town, out West, was due back in D.C. later that day.

"Vince didn't join his colleagues," Linda remembered. "With a slow gait, he hung back silently, watching nothing in particular." It really bothered her. President Clinton confirmed Linda's recollection of "Foster standing at the back, near one of the grand old magnolia trees planted by Andrew Jackson." The difference was that President Clinton was not bothered.

"Vince had a smile on his face," he wrote in his memoir, *My Life*, "and I remember thinking he must be relieved that he and the counsel's office were working on things like Supreme Court and FBI appointments, instead of answering endless questions about the travel office."[37]

Judge Freeh, who left his lifetime appointment on the federal bench to head the bureau, made a brief acceptance speech: "At its bedrock, the FBI must stand for absolute integrity, be free of all political influence … and work solely in the public interest."[38]

By 9:40 a.m., the ceremony was over. The stewards began breaking down the chairs while the press corps filed reports.

Inside the White House, the ongoing interior refurbishing and restorations costing north of $300,000, "to ensure the upkeep of the Executive Mansion as a living museum," which was directed by Hillary, banged away.[39]

President Clinton and Vice President Gore returned to their offices, and the staffers went back to their desks.

At 10:30 a.m., Foster stepped out of his office, without an explanation. Nor did he offer one when he returned. None of the five Foster investigations could pinpoint where he went. *To get the gun?*

At approximately 11:00 a.m., Gorham (Foster's assistant) hung her purse over her shoulder, and got ready to run out to pick up notary papers for Hillary.

When she reached this point in her narrative, Linda visibly stiffened as she frequently did when Hillary entered our conversations. She recounted how Gorham was always running out for Hillary. ("Vince wanted her to become a notary to save time," Linda noted.) But this time, Gorham's leaving was different. Support staff covered for one another, practically every day, but Gorham asked her to specifically look out for Foster, which struck Linda as unusual. After verifying that his afternoon calendar was clear, Gorham asked her to remind him to eat lunch if she wasn't back in time.

"Why would she ask you to remind Vince to eat?" I asked her.

"Because he was a workaholic, he worked from dawn till dusk," Linda explained, "and often skipped meals."

The White House cafeteria, known as the "mess," could take up to twenty-five minutes to prepare your

26

order. At close to noon, Linda was getting hungry. She popped her head into Foster's office.

"Hungry?" she asked, startling him. Foster looked up from his papers, hesitated, then answered, "Yeah, umm cheeseburger, fries, and a Coke. Thanks."

About ten minutes later, Linda and Betsy Pond left for the "mess," leaving White House intern Tom Castleton alone with Foster. "I was very clear," Linda insisted. "I told Tom we'd be right back, and not to leave. He was the only one to get the phones."

Shortly thereafter, Linda and Betsy were in the mess line carrying their trays when Linda poured a boatload of M&Ms on Foster's tray hoping to cheer him up, since M&Ms were his favorites. Then out of nowhere and out of breath Castleton was standing behind her.

"Tom, what are you doing here?" Linda asked the intern. A member of support staff was required to be with a lawyer in the counsel's office. Office protocol.

"Vince sent me to get his lunch," Castleton responded.

It did not make sense to her since Foster, who often forgot to eat, knew how long it took to get lunch. Even more unusual, why would Foster send the remaining staff person out of the office? *Could he have contemplated taking his life then?*

Back at the counsel's office, Foster was waiting at the entrance when they returned upstairs. Linda joked as she handed him his lunch tray. "You must be very hungry to have sent Tom down," and asked again if he was all right.

Vince shuffled his feet, muttering excuses under his breath, claiming he was just hungry, "That's all, thought it was taking a lot of time," he said brushing off her concerns.

I saw Linda, almost instinctively, glance at her watch, as she must have done that day with Vince, reliving it. "I kidded him, 'A lot of time, Vince? You know how long it takes. Are you sure you're all right?'"

But Vince made up another excuse, his head hung heavy, "It's okay, I was just looking for my lunch."

He took his tray into his office, and sat on the loveseat facing his desk, absently flipping through a newspaper, with his back toward the staffers. Linda could not help but periodically look over. Vince normally was on the phone, working on a brief, talking into his Dictaphone, loaded with work, and never enough time. "I can't recall him sitting quietly eating lunch before," Linda said. It was not quite 1:00 p.m.

Minutes later, Linda was barely halfway through her lunch when Vince appeared in the counsel's suite. Smiling broadly, he told her, "Help yourself. There are a lot of M&Ms left." Before she could open her mouth, he hit the door, quickly adding, "I'll be back."

"That was it." Linda said to me, miserably, repeating it, "That was it." That was the last time she saw Vince Foster alive.

Linda was startled by his quick departure because she could not imagine where he was going. There were no appointments in his closely kept calendar. Then a funny feeling hit her in the pit of her stomach, but she threw it off. Going into his office to grab some M&Ms, she found he had eaten maybe one. He had removed the onions from his burger but had not eaten it all. For someone so anxious to eat, one would have thought he would have finished his lunch. *From the autopsy report: "It appeared that the victim had eaten a "large meal" which might have been meat and potatoes."*[40]

Later that afternoon, Gorham returned from her errands, stymied and kept saying, "There's nothing on the book. Where did Vince go?"

"All I could say was he wouldn't say," Linda said, shrugging her shoulders. "He looked like he had an appointment. Maybe he was meeting someone in the building."

More than two hours passed. Now it was after 3:00 p.m., and the counsel's office hummed with its usual heavy workload. Nussbaum and the other lawyers had long returned from lunch, but there was still no word from Foster. C. Brantley Buck, Foster's former partner at the Rose Law Firm where he had worked with Hillary, called in to discuss the Clintons' blind trust they had been setting up together. Gordon Rather, a Little Rock attorney, and others within the White House, also dialed in looking for Foster on "routine calls" when Linda remembered Nussbaum paging him.[41] "They were rarely out of contact and it was not like Vince not to check in. Bernie was concerned." Linda said.

The day after Foster's body was found in Fort Marcy Park, White House Chief of Communications Director Mark Gearan was asked at a press briefing, "Was it unusual for [Foster] to be out of the office all afternoon? ... Did he say anything to anyone before he left the White House?"

"He did not," Gearan answered. "He said he would be back. At different points during the day Bernie said, 'Is he back yet?' But it was not atypical."[42]

Two other reporters pressed for more. "Was anyone in the office alarmed?" Each time Gearan reiterated, "From visiting with Bernie, he did say ["Is Vince back yet?"], from time to time and then by the end of the day, they thought he might have then returned home. It was not necessarily atypical ... It was not viewed as any way unusual ... They weren't sure of his exact schedule."[43]

When questioned as to whether or not there was concern for Foster's welfare in the counsel's office, Gearan answered: "No."

But that was not true.

"Think about it—what job doesn't require their staff checking in?" Linda countered, "This is the White House. Staff, especially senior staff, always remain in touch. They have to. You never know when something of world consequence may occur." Growing visibly annoyed, she reinforced her argument disputing the White House's official version, "Deb always knew Vince's schedule, just like I knew Bernie's. Even support staff—all of us had to coordinate our schedules so someone was in the office. No, what Mark said wasn't true. I can't remember how many times Bernie and Deb asked about Vince. It's outrageous and insulting that the White House would suggest otherwise," Linda exclaimed. "We racked our brains trying to figure out where Vince went, and tried to find him. I was running out of logical excuses, worried myself. We all were."

"So when the reporter asked if someone paged Vince or tried to reach him, and Mark answered, 'No,' is that true?" I asked Linda.[44]

"No. Bernie paged Vince," she said.

Worried, from what Linda observed, Nussbaum was concerned for a while. She reiterated again how they weren't merely colleagues but friends, "almost brothers," and workaholics, who relied heavily on one another and were rarely out of touch.

"Was Mark in the counsel's office that day?" I asked.

"Not that I know of," Linda replied.

"So, his press briefing is not a first-hand account. Is it fair to say Mark may not have known?" I asked.

"Possible," she conceded. "He was following orders. No one who speaks on behalf of the White House goes before the press until they're briefed on what to say. He told the press what the Clintons wanted the public to hear."

Linda was not the only person who recalled the White House paging Foster, according to Betsy Pond's Park Police interview, Pond recalled paging Foster herself and leaving the White House number for him to call back.[45]

The issue as to whether or not Nussbaum or anyone else inside the White House paged Foster may seem small, even irrelevant, but it was not irrelevant to the White House, which initially denied it had happened.

According to a U.S. Park Police evidence control receipt, Foster's pager, discovered in the off position, was attached to the belt he was wearing when his body was found.[46] Other personal property, such as his wallet, rings, and watch, were released to the White House on the evening of July 21 to be returned to his family. [47] Typically, the next of kin is given the deceased's personal belongings *after* a thorough investigation is conducted to rule out any question of foul play. The handling of Foster's belongings—forensically un-tested, unique—fed the conspiracy beast. It could never be proven whether it was Foster or somebody else who turned off his pager. Finger-prints were not lifted off any of his personal belongings either.

Four years after Foster's death, Starr found, "White House records of pager messages do not indicate messages sent to or from Mr. Foster," a finding which would negate Linda and Betsy Pond's memory, except later in Starr's report we learned that, "complete [White House] records ... are not available."[48] *Why would the White House withhold records?*

Starr was not alone in his frustrated attempt to obtain documentation from the Clinton White House. The Senate Whitewater Committee ran into the same obstacle during their investigation.

Two-and-a-half years after Foster's death, on January 22, 1996, the committee found "because the testimony of witnesses ... was often contradictory, the committee has placed particular emphasis on available documentary evidence. Unfortunately, the committee has been hindered by parties unduly delaying the production of, or withholding outright, documents critical to [the Foster] investigation."[49]

Was Linda telling the truth? Did Bernie page Vince? It's a possibility and cannot be ruled out. What was the big deal about admitting to paging a colleague who was out of the office when no one knew where he was? Moreover, isn't withholding documents under subpoena called "obstruction of justice"?

For Linda and Deb it had been a long day. And, unbeknownst to them, July 20, 1993, was far from over. In fact, it was just beginning. Late afternoon, the ladies left the president's lawyers in the counsel's office and headed for home. By then, Lisa, Foster's wife, had called in looking for her husband, but there still was no word from him.

Linda left Bernie with no out-of-office meetings scheduled on his calendar that night. Considering the lawyers' workload dealing with the Clinton scandals, including Travelgate, the mess with the FBI, and Supreme Court vetting troubles (Zoe Baird's and Kimba Wood's Attorney General nominations imploded after it was revealed they had employed illegal aliens), Linda was surprised if the president's lawyers were lucky enough to go home before 10:00 p.m.[50]

Foster, like his counsel office colleagues, began work between "7:30 and 8:30 a.m. and worked until 9:30 p.m. or later, either six or seven days per week."[51]

At 5:59 p.m., Francis Swann, a park service employee, contacted 911 and reported that a possible dead body had been found in Fort Marcy Park.[52] Inside the Clinton White House, at minimum, senior staffers were at work at the time of Foster's death. Mid-flight to

D.C. from the West Coast, Hillary made an abrupt and unscheduled stop in Arkansas "between 8:00 and 9:00 p.m.," as she wrote in her book, *Living History*, "to drop off [her] mother and visit some friends."[53]

# 3

# The Foster Investigations

"Do not turn to the right or the left;
remove your foot from evil."

**—Proverbs 4:27 (NKJV)**

Imagine being the president of the United States, or the First Lady, and discovering that your friend, your best friend, was found dead in a park. More than a valued colleague, he had grieved with you when your father had died.[54] He had celebrated your White House victory. He had been your rock of Gibraltar and uprooted his life and his family from the place he grew up to serve in your administration in Washington.[55] His wife taught your daughter how to swim in their backyard pool. His children were your child's friends.[56]

Let's assume you have the good fortune to sit in America's highest office with advantages the average person doesn't enjoy—unlimited access to top investigative offices, the CIA and FBI, the world's top experts one-phone call away. With the stroke of a pen you had issued executive orders that overturned statutes. But instead of using this power, these resources, to find out everything about your friend's death, you leave it to the U.S. Park Police to investigate before anyone could know with reasonable confidence that no foul play was involved. Oddly, during five investigations spanning four years, the Clinton White House never turned over documents that investigators sought to help them do their jobs. And, if someone challenged the official findings, and held hearings like the "Republican senators and their staffs conducted," on Foster's death, as Hillary wrote in her book, *Living History*, they "inflicted great emotional and monetary damage on innocent people."[57]

Individuals with fewer resources have done more to find out everything there was to know about the sudden and shocking death of a friend or loved one, than did the Clintons for their "dear" friend. Some of their stories appear on shows like NBC's *Dateline*, ABC's *20/20* and *Primetime Live*, CBS's *48 Hour Mystery;* and on *Fox News, CNN,* and *MSNBC.*

By contrast, consider the history of the Foster investigations.

Two days after Foster died, Press Secretary Dee Dee Myers told the press about the U.S. Park Police investigation—the first investigation. "Well, just to be clear, what [the Park Police] are really looking for is just anything that would confirm that it was a suicide ... It is a fairly limited investigation," she said, "the Park Service is just looking into—again to establish—to confirm what they believe was a suicide." When pressed for more information, Myers reiterated the Clinton White House talking points, "My only point is that at this point, the Park Service Police is the only agency that's investigating, and that the objective of their search is simply to determine that it was a suicide."[58]

From the get-go, homicide, foul play, the possibility of blackmail, a potential risk to national security, were never investigated. As a government official, principally one who worked directly with the First Family, it is reasonable to assume and expect that a closer look was warranted.

Because Foster apparently died in a National Park,

the case belonged to the Park Police, part of the Department of the Interior. The FBI—which normally would have and could have investigated such a death—was sidelined. As Myers affirmed, "There's no other federal agencies that are investigating."

Next, Linda's boss, Nussbaum, on behalf of the counsel's office, requested that the Justice Department coordinate Foster's investigation with the Park Police.[59] It sounded good.

But one week later, "the Justice Department backed off its pledge to conduct a full investigation" and said "it was merely participating in a low-level inquiry" run by the Park Police.[60] The Park Police concluded Foster committed suicide in Fort Marcy Park.

The second investigation began nearly six months after Foster's death, on January 20, 1994. Under pressure from Congress and the press, Attorney General Reno appointed Independent Counsel Robert Fiske Jr. to launch an investigation in conjunction with the ongoing Whitewater investigations. Whitewater (the Whitewater Development Company, Inc.) had become news on the 1992 campaign trail. It was then that the Clintons claimed Whitewater (a parcel of land they had purchased in 1978 in Arkansas to develop vacation homes with Jim and Susan McDougal, while Bill was Attorney General) was simply a $68,000 money-losing venture. The controversy faded until the press began poking around at "the relationship between the Clintons," and "the banking activity at two McDougal-controlled financial institutions—Madison Bank & Trust and Madison Guaranty Savings & Loan Association,"—and Hillary's legal counsel role with the Rose Law Firm. In 1986 Madison Guaranty failed, costing U.S. taxpayers $73 million to bail out.[61] Eventually, both McDougals were convicted of fraud.[62]

Fiske released his report on the death of Vince

Foster on June 30, 1994, agreeing with the Park Police's assessment. On February 24, 1994, seven months after Foster's death, Republican Congressman William F. Clinger Jr. initiated his inquiry. It was the third Foster investigation. Clinger released his report on August 12, 1994, endorsing the Park Police findings based on "all the available facts."[63]

Next it was the Senate Banking Committee's turn—the fourth Foster investigation. The bipartisan committee, also known as the Senate Whitewater Committee, held hearings on July 29, 1994.[64]

Fourteen months after Foster's death, on August 5, 1994, the fifth and final investigation began when newly appointed Kenneth Starr's Independent Counsel launched an inquiry.

It's vital to point out here that before the first OIC investigation was completed, on March 5, 1994, Linda's boss, Nussbaum, resigned from the counsel's office in humiliated disgrace for his mishandling of the Whitewater and the Foster investigations.[65] Shortly thereafter, on March 14, 1994, Webster Hubbell, who with Foster worked closely with Hillary at the Rose Law Firm in Arkansas, resigned from the Justice Department—also disgraced and then indicted. (Hubbell pleaded guilty to tax evasion and fraud that December. During the sixteen months after Hubbell's resignation, he received seventeen consulting contracts totaling over $450,000 from supporters of President Clinton. While the Independent Counsel found that Hubbell "did little or no work for the money paid by his consulting clients," he determined there was insufficient evidence to conclude that the money was intended to influence Hubbell's cooperation with investigators in the Whitewater investigation).[66] Both men, long-time Clinton friends and colleagues, had been questioned in the investigations.

Two years after Foster's death, in 1995, the Senate Whitewater Committee "overwhelmingly" affirmed Fiske's second conclusion, which concurred with the Park Police's first investigation.[67] On October 10, 1997, four years after Foster died, Starr concurred with Fiske's conclusion, which also affirmed the Park Police's investigation. Indeed, Foster committed suicide in Fort Marcy Park. He was depressed. Case closed, so it seemed.

Except the problems with the Park Police's initial investigation (the foundation for the next four investigations) began instantly; and immediately raised unanswered questions.

For openers, evidence gathering where Foster's body was found was at best poorly handled, as Starr wrote, "The collection and preservation of physical evidence is [sic] the most important building blocks available to the crime scene investigator."[68] In Foster's case, the 35mm photographs that Park Police took of his body "were underexposed and of little value."[69] Because Foster's "clothing was packaged together before trace evidence was collected, specific trace evidence cannot be conclusively linked to particular items of clothing [that Foster] was wearing at the time of his death. To obtain precise trace evidence analyses, each item must be kept separate before trace evidence is collected."[70] The medical examiner's laboratory "intended to take x-rays" of Foster's body but the lab's new x-ray machine was "not functioning properly."[71] No alternative arrangements were made. Foster was buried three days after he died.

"A perfect reconstruction ... was not possible," wrote Dr. Henry Lee, famed Director of the Connecticut State Police Forensic Science Laboratory, when he was commissioned by Starr to help in his investigation. Lee, known for the O.J. Simpson case, wrote: "The reasons include the lack of complete documentation of the original shooting scene; the lack of subsequent records and photographs of each item of physical evidence prior to examinations; the lack of documentation of the amount of blood, tissue, and bone fragments in the areas at the scene under and around Foster's head; the lack of close-up photographs of any definite patterns and quantity of the blood stains on Foster's clothing and body at the scene; and the unknown location of the fatal bullet, which makes complete reconstruction of the bullet trajectory difficult."[72]

Based on the Park Police's failure at evidence gathering, common sense would say there was only one reasonable and solid conclusion that all the Foster inquiries should have reached: it was not possible to decisively conclude what had happened to Vince Foster.

Both Starr and Fiske attempted to recover evidence and complete what the original investigation had missed or failed to do. Starr sent investigators to the neighborhood around Fort Marcy Park because there was "no record of any effort to canvass the neighborhood near the time of death to determine whether anyone had seen or heard relevant information."[73]

Another failed attempt brought Fiske and Starr's investigators back to the park to locate physical evidence, specifically bone fragments from Foster's skull and the fatal bullet that four Park Police investigators had unsuccessfully tried to locate two days after Foster's death by using a "metal detector" in the immediate area where his body was found. OIC investigators recovered bullets and other metal objects, but none of the bullets was the one that killed Foster. During Fiske's inquiry, agents screened and sifted through approximately 18 inches down into the soil, and found "no bone fragments" that belonged to Foster.[74]

Taking into account the indisputable failures of the Park Police's unreliable investigation, who had confidently accepted the official Foster findings? Bill and Hillary Clinton. Did Linda trust those findings?

"No, of course not. How can anyone trust it? That's why it's so chilling," she answered. "The official version is what the Clintons wanted everyone to believe."[75]

Bill Clinton wrote in *My Life* that he "was glad Fiske was looking at [Foster's death]. The scandal machine was trying to get blood out of a turnip and maybe this would shut them up and give Vince's family some relief."[76]

When Foster's death fell under Starr's purview, President Clinton grew impatient: "Starr showed his 'independence' when unbelievably he said he was going to reinvestigate Vince Foster's death."[77] In 957 pages of President Clinton's memoir, there are no references of concern or outrage over the outrageously flawed evidence gathering done by the Park Police regarding the death of his childhood friend.

For Hillary, like her husband, the official Foster findings are untouchable. There were also no references of concern or outrage over the flawed evidence gathering in 538 pages of Hillary's memoir regarding the death of her closest confidante. When it came to Starr, Hillary described him as the "part-timer; [with] zero criminal law experience, who was learning on the job."[78] Yet she was satisfied when, as she wrote in her book, "Starr had finally conceded that Vince Foster really had committed suicide. (Robert Fiske had reached that conclusion three years earlier, but it took four more official investigations, including Starr's, to confirm it.)"[79] Why would the "part-timer with zero criminal law experience" be trusted now?

It should have taken one competent investigation to resolve a senior White House official's death and end reasonable speculation. Instead, Bill and Hillary deemed the "official findings" as truth based on the Park Police's slapdash investigative work.

But placing culpability entirely on the Park Police would be unfair. Like their successors, they confronted strong-armed, obstruction-like tactics from the Clinton White House. According to Thomas Collier, the chief of staff of the secretary of the Interior, "The Park Police" were "very, very, upset about the investigation … [and] that they really couldn't get the cooperation [from the White House] that they wanted to their superiors."[80]

As the Senate Whitewater Committee reported after their initial hearings were held: "… the Special Committee concludes that senior White House officials, particularly members of the Office of the White House Counsel, engaged in a pattern of highly improper conduct … following [Foster's] death. These senior White House officials deliberately prevented career law enforcement officers from the Department of Justice and Park Police from fully investigating the circumstances surrounding Mr. Foster's death, including whether he took his own life because of troubling matters involving the President and Mrs. Clinton."[81]

The passage of time in any investigation is never kind. Leads run cold. Memories fade. Forensic evidence vanishes. One cannot undo the bungled evidence-collecting that initially occurred. Neither Starr nor Fiske, despite their attempts, could turn back time and re-collect precious evidence where Foster's body was found or where he was last seen alive. Forced to draw a conclusion from the incomplete evidence they had, the OIC investigators had no alternative but to draw the most logical explanation.

To solve Foster's death with confidence would require securing missing evidence, a smoking gun of sorts, a confession. History has shown that it is possible. Confessions and bouts of good conscience have solved cold cases before. It took eighteen years of exhaustive FBI inquiries for Ted Kaczynski, the Unabomber, to be caught and that was only after his brother came forward.[82] In December 2002, the defendants who pled guilty thirteen years earlier to brutally raping and nearly killing the Central Park jogger were released from prison in part because of a confession and DNA.[83] In 2012, new information surfaced regarding front-runner presidential candidate of the Democratic Party Robert F. Kennedy's 1968 assassination when an eyewitness stepped forward and claimed that Sirhan Sirhan did not act alone, "The truth has got to come out. No more cover-ups," the witness insisted. The case has since been re-opened.[84]

Soon I would learn that the lingering, troublesome questions in the Foster case could be answered; that the nagging suspicions that Linda was hiding something, when I attempted to report her story accurately, were absolutely right. Time showed me that just because Kenneth Starr's OIC arrived at the same conclusion as the other investigations (by using the same limited, contaminated, and "available evidence" they had) did not mean their conclusions were accurate.[85]

# 4

# Rigor-Mortis

"Then the eyes of those who see will no longer be closed,
and the ears of those who hear will listen."

**—Isaiah 32:3 (NIV)**

Linda was in traffic heading for home on the evening
of July 20, 1993, when a man referred to as Confidential
Witness (CW), pulled into Fort Marcy Park, "one of a
ring of fortifications constructed during the Civil War to
defend Washington against a Confederate attack,"
located about six and a half miles from downtown
Washington.[86]

It was approximately 5:45 p.m., more than an hour
and a half before the sun set on that clear night at 7:30
p.m.[87] Evidently needing to relieve himself, CW
"following a path off the parking lot for approximately
200 yards" near one of two cannons, started climbing an
embankment, when he eyed what he initially assumed
was a pile of trash by the barrel of one cannon. Taking a
closer look, he stood at the top of the berm and realized
he was wrong. It was not trash. He was standing just
above the head of a [man's] body.[88] The man was
"dressed in a white dress shirt, expensive trousers, and
black dress shoes."[89]

At first, CW nearly walked away "thinking someone was taking a nap," but the blood on the man's lips
and nostrils, some of it "dry and black," grabbed his

attention and he froze in his tracks. CW observed that "the man's face was straight up. His hands lay straight against each side of his body, as if he'd just lain down.[90] His eyes traveled downwards towards the man's hands and stopped. The man's hands were empty; his "palms were facing upwards." CW did not see a gun in his hands.[91]

His eyes traveled further downwards, now CW was looking at the densely overgrown foliage, the accumulation of leaves from years of neglect … that surrounded his body, "but the leaves from just about his waist down to the bottom of the forty-five degree slope … had all been tramped down as though someone had walked back and forth at least a dozen times."[92] *Was the man murdered? Were the culprits still there?*

Robert Fiske found CW to be credible.
"CW provided details that have never become public, and that could only have been known by the person who discovered Foster's body." [93]
Eight years later, in 2001, in a radio interview on WABC's *John Bachelor and Paul Alexander Show*, CW recounted, "Till this day, I felt like I interrupted someone putting [Foster] there, and there was someone there point blank when I was there," he said. "Because that gun did not fall out of a tree … Someone put that gun in his hand."[94]
Fiske reasoned that CW must have been mistaken about the gun that was later found at the scene in Foster's hand: "… it was difficult to see [Foster's] hands because of the dense foliage in the area where the body was lying." But CW refuted Fiske's rationale and called it "a point blank lie." Having "zero doubt," he detailed the reasons why he noticed the trampled leaves in the first place. He was "looking to see if the man had

something in his hands." He was looking to see if something that the man once had in his hands had fallen or rolled down the bank. "That's what made my eyes follow down the embankment," CW said. [95]

Seeing no gun, no rock, no sign of a weapon, CW rushed to his van, and drove nearly two miles to the parkway maintenance facility, where he reported the dead body to two off-duty Park Service workers who were drinking beer. One Park Service worker called 911, followed by a call to the Park Police and CW left the park and went home.[96]

It was not until the following day when CW learned that the unidentified body he had found was Vince Foster Jr., deputy counsel to the president of the United States Bill Clinton.

At 6:09 p.m., Emergency Medical Services (EMS) arrived at Fort Marcy Park, followed by Park Police investigator John Rolla, who at "approximately 6:35 p.m." was one of the first investigators to arrive. [97] He had "observed that some of the blood on Foster's face was still wet, but starting to dry. [Rolla] touched Foster's body, and noted it was still relatively warm, and there was no sign of rigor mortis." [98]

Typically, the onset of rigor mortis begins in the facial musculature area of the body, and is evident two to four hours or longer after death. However, rigor mortis may begin as early as ten minutes after death, "depending on the condition of the body at death and on factors in the atmosphere, particularly temperature."[99] Heat accelerates the onset of rigor mortis while cold impedes it. The "ninety degree heat that day," according to Starr, would be linked in part to explain Foster's warm body temperature, yet that theory should also apply to the wet blood on his face which should've dried quickly under those circumstances. Investigators indicated there was very little blood around Foster's body and face—a piece of evidence supported by CW, who also "saw no blood splatter, no pool of blood" (an unexplained abnormality for a self-inflicted gunshot wound to the mouth). Yet, for reasons never explained, none of the investigations could pinpoint Foster's time of death.[100]

According to the National Oceanic and Atmospheric administration (NOAA), July 20, 1993, was an unusually dry and hot day with zero precipitation. At 5:50 p.m., the approximate time when Foster's body was discovered, the temperature had barely dropped from the day's high of 96 degrees to a sizzling 92 degrees. At 6:50 p.m., the sun would not set for another forty minutes when the temperature dropped to 90 degrees.[101]

On a hot day, with dry, brittle conditions, is it reasonable to conclude that Foster's blood would have dried rapidly and facial musculature rigor mortis would begin early? If so, did Foster die shortly before his body was discovered?

———

Elizabeth "Lisa" Braden Foster, Foster's wife of twenty-five years, and mother to their three children (two sons and a daughter), nearly collapsed when Park Police agents Cheryl Braun and John Rolla told her of her husband's fate. Shocked, devastated, and overwhelmed, at first she thought they meant her son, Vincent Jr., was dead, not her husband.[102]

It was approximately 10:10 p.m. when the agents arrived at 3027 Cambridge Place N.W., the home she shared with her husband, in Georgetown, Washington, D.C. White House operation director and Arkansas friend David Watkins and his wife accompanied the investigators when they delivered the grim news.[103]

Web Hubbell, who arrived at the same time with

Foster's sisters, Sheila and Sharon, told investigators he was paged with the bad news while dining at a Lebanese Tavern.[104] Other White House staffers who came that night were: Bruce Lindsey, William Kennedy, Marsha Scott, David Gergen, and Chelsea's nanny, Helen Dickey. Foster's family and family friends, Senator Pryor, Vernon Jordan, Walter and Mrs. Pincus also gathered together while they struggled to "make logic out of [Foster's] death."[105]

That night was "the only time" Press Secretary Dee Dee Myers remembered President Clinton leaving the White House without the press.[106]

About an hour later, a Secret Service detail pulled up and escorted the president accompanied by Chief of Staff Mack McLarty into Foster's home.

"I tried to console everyone, but I was hurting too, and feeling, as I had when Frank Aller killed himself, angry at Vince for doing it and angry at myself for not seeing it coming and doing something, anything, to try and stop it," wrote President Clinton in his book, *My Life*. "I was also sad for all my friends from Arkansas who had come to Washington wanting nothing more than to serve and do good only to find their every move second-guessed. Now Foster, the tall, handsome, strong, and self-assured person they felt was the most stable of them all, was gone."[107]

Investigator Rolla testified that no one at Foster's home that night had "seen this coming." All of his friends, colleagues, and family members—those who did speak to investigators, provided "negative answers;" Foster was not depressed and no one knew if he had been taking any anti-depression medications.[108]

The next day at a press briefing President Clinton said, "For more years than most of us like to admit, in times of difficulty [Foster] was normally the Rock of

Gibraltar while other people were having trouble. No one could remember the reverse being the case."[109]

When asked by a White House reporter whether Foster might have felt blame or guilt for things that went wrong during the first six months of the Clinton administration referring to Travelgate, Whitewater, Hillary-Care, and the failed nanny-gate attorney general nominees, President Clinton answered: "I don't think so. I certainly don't think that can explain it, and I certainly don't think it's accurate."

Mark Gearan reinforced President Clinton's sentiment later at another White House press briefing, "I can only repeat what I've said in that there was nothing people felt that [Foster] said anything in the extraordinary that was out of the ordinary to his colleagues or to his friends. Something we've all thought about."[110]

The media didn't buy it. Skepticism and disbelief from the press triggered the first of what would become a pattern of Clinton White House reversals that were issued after Foster's death. About a week later, the chorus of public statements from the White House initially claiming Foster was fine, no one saw suicide coming, dramatically switched to Vince was very, very troubled.

Linda remembered Hillary's original cohesive strategy, crafted in the counsel's office after Foster's death, which was delivered from the White House press room as 'talking points' to the public (where staffers are told exactly what happened and are briefed on what to say, creating the "truth" until it became the so-called truth) had to be revised from, "Found dead in Fort Marcy Park, suicide, we didn't see it coming," to "Found dead in Fort Marcy Park, suicide, Vince was depressed."

Now her boss, Nussbaum, suddenly recalled, "Foster's work effort decreased noticeably."[111] Others abruptly remembered that he "had seemed distressed."

As the *New York Times* reported over a week after the White House's initial response, "In contrast to White House assertions that there had been no signs of trouble, Vincent W. Foster Jr., the longtime friend of President Clinton who apparently committed suicide last week, had displayed signs of depression in the final month of his life, according to Federal officials and people close to Mr. Foster. Mr. Foster ... had been so depressed about his job that before his death he had spent parts of several weekends working reclusively at home in bed with the shades drawn, a close associate said today."[112]

About seventy minutes after arriving at the Foster home the evening of July 20, 1993, Park Police investigators Braun and Rolla were asked to leave. The agents were told that the family was too distraught to answer questions; nevertheless before they left Foster's home, they asked David Watkin's to notify the Secret Service to seal off Foster's White House office—that proper procedural request was not carried out. [113]

Instead of securing Foster's White House office— where he was last seen alive, there was security around Foster's home, with chief of White House personnel security Craig Livingston remaining on watch outside. Livingston was a former bar bouncer from Arkansas, whose prior qualifications for his important, sensitive White House job included combating pesky teenagers with fake ids, and belligerent drunks. In 1996 Livingston would resign in disgrace for improperly obtaining hundreds of Federal Bureau of Investigations security clearances of Republicans that illegally ended up in the West Wing during the Clinton Filegate investigation.[114]

One person who was visibly absent from Foster's

home that night was his senior partner, and "almost-brother," Nussbaum. This was news to Linda who became visibly disturbed when I noted her boss's absence.

"I can't imagine why he wouldn't be with Vince's family. Are you sure?" she said to me, clearly troubled and asked me to double check. I did and Nussbaum was not there. "What could have been more important to keep him away from Vince's family?" she mumbled out loud, almost to herself. "I just can't believe Bernie left the office until he heard from Vince. He was so worried about him."

Linda stood up, began pacing and she looked silently out the living room window.

Apparently, what was more important than being with Foster's family was a celebration dinner followed by a visit to Foster's unsealed White House office.

Nussbaum, like Foster, worked long and demanding hours at the White House. Typically, he "left the office at 8:00 or 9:00 or 10:00 p.m." each night.[115] The day Foster went missing and then was found dead was an exception to Nussbaum's characteristically long workday schedule.

Nussbaum told investigators he went to the White House from a Washington restaurant, Galileo's, after learning Foster was dead shortly after nine o'clock. He had been enjoying a celebratory dinner, toasting Freeh's nomination to helm the FBI.[116] However, Nussbaum's statement conflicts with White House records that indicated he entered the premises at 10:48 p.m. Oddly, records do not show at what time Nussbaum had left the White House earlier to go out and celebrate.

In the same way that problems occurred during the Park Police's investigation where Foster's body was found, problems for investigators inside the White House where Foster was last seen alive surfaced immediately, never stopped, and are disturbing to this day.

Nussbaum told investigators that because President Clinton was appearing on CNN's *Larry King Live*, he (Nussbaum) went directly to Foster's office to look for a suicide note and to notify other staffers. When he reached the counsel's office, Nussbaum said he saw a light inside Foster's office. When he walked in, he bumped into long-time Clinton friend, director of administration Patsy Thomasson (a staffer who was working in the West Wing despite not having a security clearance, and who was also involved in the travel office investigation), with Hillary's chief of staff Maggie Williams—both were at Foster's desk.[117] Williams claimed she had gone to Foster's office, hoping to find him alive.[118] (During the Clintons campaign finance scandal investigation, dubbed "Chinagate," Williams accepted $50,000 cash from Johnny Chung in the White House.[119] She left the White House after Bill Clinton's first term, according to Hillary, because she "wanted her life back," and left Washington with her husband to move to Paris."[120] She later served as Hillary's presidential campaign manager in Hillary's 2008 failed presidential bid.)[121] The three senior staffers innocently claimed they were all looking for a suicide note, yet the trio's hunt proved fruitless. It would take six days to find what the White House would later describe as Foster's suicide "note."

Amazingly, a seasoned top-notch attorney, Hillary's chief of staff, and the White House director of administration all failed to think that it might have been a good idea to secure Foster's office, and all three shared strikingly different accounts of what transpired inside it. The discrepancies were vast, ever-changing, and sparked a debate that was never resolved.[122]

As the Senate Whitewater Committee investigation found, "Time and again, the testimony of career law enforcement officials and others without a motive to lie, as well as documentary evidence, told one consistent story, while senior White House officials and close Clinton associates offered a contradictory version of the facts."

Hillary's senior aides and close confidantes could not agree as to who entered Foster's office first, and who did what inside. Then they attributed their conflicting accounts to grief and "I-can't-remember" amnesia-like testimony. Even more disturbing, Nussbaum could not settle on the time he spent alone searching through Foster's office. His account varied from ten minutes to two hours, handing another plateful of contradictions and dubious behavior for the conspiracy beast to chew on. [123]

# 5

# There is Blood in that Turnip

"Do not say, 'A conspiracy,' concerning all that this people
call a conspiracy, nor be afraid of their threats,
nor be troubled."

**—Isaiah 8:12 (NJKV)**

Upstairs at Linda Tripp's Maryland home.

It was near midnight on July 20, 1993, when the loud ringing phone jolted Linda awake from a deep slumber. Foster's body had been found in Fort Marcy Park less than six hours earlier. A shaky Deb Coyle, who had worked with President Bill Clinton outside the Oval office, was on the line. Apparently, the ladies had been close when they worked together outside the Oval, occasionally hanging out after hours. However, that all changed when Linda was transferred to work for Nussbaum in Hillary's counsel's office, and she said she had not spoken to Coyle since then.

"Linda, it's Deb. Wake up."

"What, Deb, I'm aslee—" Linda barely mumbled.
"Linda. Wake up! Vince is dead," Coyle cried out.
Bolting upwards in disbelief, Linda was immediately alert. "What!?"
"He's dead, Linda," Deb said. "They found Vince's body in Fort Marcy Park with a bullet wound to his

head. It was suicide. He committed suicide."[124]

"He whaaaat?" Linda shouted disbelievingly.

"Vince committed suicide," Deb repeated herself.

But Linda had seen Foster alive less than eleven hours earlier. The investigation had barely begun, yet the White House was notifying staffers with specifics: Foster committed suicide in Fort Marcy Park.

"It was too soon for the White House to know what happened," Linda maintained. "They could've told us he was found dead in the park. 'Looks like a suicide … we're investigating.' But no, they wanted me, all the staffers, and the American people to believe their version, now."

Linda had a big point. Typically whenever a scandal broke, Bill and Hillary cautioned the public to wait until the facts came out before drawing any conclusions. Their reaction to Foster's death was the exact opposite.

During the Lewinsky-Clinton scandal, for example, Hillary said, "that the best thing to do in these cases is just to be patient, take a deep breath, and the truth will come out."[125]

Bill wanted evidence during Filegate (another Clinton investigation where hundreds of FBI files in a "bureaucratic snafu" ended up in the Clinton White House), "Until I have evidence to the contrary—and I mean evidence," the president said, "…we need evidence before we draw any conclusions."[126]

Instead of waiting for *the evidence* to be gathered in Foster's death investigation, here is what the Clinton White House told the public.

The night of July 20, 1993, the White House issued a statement announcing Foster's body was discovered in Fort Marcy Park, near the George Washington Parkway in Virginia. "The positive identification of Mr. Foster's body was provided to the White House at approximately 9:55 p.m., and the death was reported by

Park Service investigators as an apparent suicide."[127]

The next day, at 12:50 p.m., before a reasonable investigation was conducted, President Clinton laid down the groundwork for the White House narrative— by presenting the cohesive strategy, the script for what would be repeated in the press and become the "truth."

At a press briefing a reporter asked the president if he had any idea why Foster might have taken his life. The president said, "No, I really don't. And, frankly, none of us do. You know, we—his closest friends sat around discussing it last night at some length. None of us do ... So I don't know if we'll ever know [what happened to Foster] ... and because no one can know why things like this happen ... *we'll just have to live with something else we can't understand* (emphasis mine)."[128]

Later that day, at a 3:30 p.m. press briefing, Chief of Staff McLarty, a friend of Foster's from Arkansas for over 40 years, parroted President Clinton: "For try as we might, all of our reason, all of our rationality, all of our logic can never answer the questions raised by such a death ... We really can never fully know a person's private pain and what might lead them in their thought process, even a person we have known all of our lives."[129]

The next day, Press Secretary Dee Dee Myers added her voice to the cohesive strategy echo chamber: "I think it's been our position that it's impossible to know ... It is a mystery, and I think the president made that very clear yesterday. It is a mystery ... you can create a whole set of objective reasons why it may have happened. But no one will ever know."[130]

Then Stephanopoulos, repeating the president, told the *Post*, "Since you can't ever know, it's impossible to speculate on it. In the end, it is a mystery."[131]

The Park Police officially declared Foster's death a suicide over two weeks later, on August 10, 1993.[132]

And Linda? "The White House ensured we would never know what happened to Vince," she curtly answered. "When President Clinton said that, he knew that part was true."

But late that July 20 night, Linda struggled to absorb Deb's incomprehensible words delivered over the phone: Vince committed suicide.

She fumbled for cigarettes on the nightstand and knocked a vase off of it. Trembling, she burst into tears and hollered, "What are you talking about? I just saw him. He can't be dead. That's not possible. Vince would never take his life. Would he?" Linda breathed in deeply, unable to wrap Deb's words around her mind, "All I could think of was why didn't I see it? What did I miss? Is it true? But, but—why? Why?"

After she hung up with Coyle, a weeping Linda dialed Deb (Gorham, Foster's assistant). Together, grief-stricken and in shock, the ladies relived the last moments they shared with Vince. Back and forth, they struggled to make sense out of the senseless and speculated on the impossible. Their imaginations ran wild and oscillated between Foster committing suicide to Foster was murdered; murder without pulling the trigger.

"I had a hard time accepting I would never see him again," Linda sorrowfully acknowledged. "I kept rejecting suicide. Wondering, if it was suicide then it had to have been his job protecting 'the client,'" a.k.a. Hillary, as Foster referred to the First Lady. Linda described how Foster, under the Clinton regime was forced to accept things against his principals.

"It was awful," Linda remembered when her tone turned deeply reflective. "The truth is none of us were happy working constant damage control for the Clintons," as she described how it was Vince who always was the person who had to clean up Hillary's messes.

Another person remembered Hillary's dealing with Foster this way: "[Hillary] would bark, 'Fix it, Vince!' or 'Handle it, Vince!' and leave him to pick up the pieces."[133]

Foster's role in the Clinton White House always bothered Linda. It should bother all Americans. Serving as counsel to the president, Foster earned a salary from taxpayers to serve the American people's interests. Instead, he represented the Clintons privately; most notably on Whitewater, their personal taxes and the travel office firings. His dubious role was not only unethical but "the possibility for conflict of interest involved in working for the Government and for a private client at the same time is so paramount a concern in the Justice Department that the department prohibits its lawyers from representing anyone privately."[134]

"Vince appeared to try to serve the American people," Linda recalled. "Like during the nominee vetting process. But every time, other, more pressing issues concerning his true client, Hillary, stole him away from his real job. Vince was completely occupied with carrying out Hillary's orders."

Even her boss, Nussbaum, acknowledged the troubling conflict of interest in Foster's White House role. "Foster tended to see himself as representing Hillary's interests," he stated in a *Time Magazine* interview three years after Foster's death. He confirmed Linda's recollection when he said "... Foster remained the Clintons' personal lawyer during his White House stint."[135]

As one Little Rock attorney later recalled about Foster, "People gravitated to Vince because he was a world-class listener. Women were drawn to him not just because he was smart and handsome, but because he seemed to keep secrets."[136]

Foster was apparently so distressed while handling the Clintons' personal affairs, as opposed to America's interests, that even his wife, Lisa, told investigators days before his death how he had "cried while talking to her on the phone." He had mentioned "resigning" from the White House.[137]

The question remains today. How can a man take his own life with a loving family, and with what *appeared* to be such a promising career that included the possibility of being appointed to the Supreme Court?[138] What was he doing for Hillary that had distressed him so?

Hyperactive speculation ran wild and politicos on both sides went bonkers. *"Murder! Foster's dead because of what he knew about the Clintons and Whitewater"* roared the Right. Republican Congressman Dan Burton of Indiana "had achieved minor celebrity for firing a .38-caliber pistol at a watermelon in his backyard as part of a bizarre attempt to prove that Vince Foster was murdered," Hillary snidely noted in her book. [139]

Meanwhile, the Left and the Clintons aimed the blame at the *Wall Street Journal*, the media, and the mystery of depression.

Foster had "been wounded by questions raised about his competence and integrity in several *Wall Street Journal* editorials … He had never been subject to public criticism before and like so many people when they're pounded in the press for the first time, he seemed to think that everyone had read the negative things said about him and believed them," Bill Clinton wrote in his memoir.[140]

Hillary wrote in hers: "Apparently, the final blow came in a series of spiteful editorials published in *The Wall Street Journal*, which attacked the integrity and competence of all the Arkansas lawyers in the Clinton administration." She believed as Foster "absorbed each accusation" from *The Wall Street Journal,* "he was driving deeper into pain and distress," and she will go to her grave "wishing" she had … "spent more time with him and had somehow seen the signs of his despair. But he was a very private person, and nobody—not his wife, Lisa … had any idea of the depth of his depression."[141]

Hanging up the phone with Deb Gorham after learning about Foster's death, Linda, not wanting Betsy Pond to hear the news on television, frantically dialed her number but there was no answer so she left an urgent message to call her when she woke up. A few minutes later, Betsy returned Linda's call. She already knew. Bernie had called her earlier and told her that Foster committed suicide in Fort Marcy Park.

I casually remarked to Linda, "Why would Bernie call Betsy and not you?" After all, Bernie Nussbaum was Linda's boss too.

She paused. It was a long pause. She was not sure. She was not pleased either. Then Linda was off and rationalizing, "Maybe Bernie called Betsy because she has a longer work history with Hillary …" she said. "Um … Bernie knew Betsy longer than he knew me … they worked together on Watergate …" Her rationalizations seemed more for her benefit then for mine.

"You know, Betsy was Bernie's secretary," Linda kept on, defensively. "I was his executive assistant."

Linda "adored" Bernie, "loved working with him," and now, unexpectedly for me, she was awfully bothered by my observation. Maybe there was no reason why. Perhaps Bernie knew Linda had already been notified. No big deal, right? Except there could be that one reason, the same reason that always sent Linda into a panic mode. She dreaded it; worried about it. What did it mean? And that reason was the White

House chain-of-command. The chain-of-command referred to who was speaking on behalf of the president, and who was speaking on behalf of the First Lady when a staffer or White House aide called from the White House. We had gone over it countless times and discussed the ramifications as to how it affected the outcome of all the investigations, and now here we were, after the fact, looking back. Then suddenly as Linda and I sat together alone in the charming living room in the guesthouse in Middleburg, Virginia, the still air stirred.

Simultaneously, it was dreadful and wonderful, vindicating and frightening. Her rationalizations deteriorated then finally tapered off to quiet, and now Linda, lost in her private thoughts, was visibly upset.

*Why would Bernie call Betsy and not you?*

She tensed up, her breath quickened when abruptly she exhaled in relief, as though a back-breaking burden were snatched off of her. Her hands caught her head cupping her chin. *Oh my God* careened through my mind, and I understood too. After all this time, all these years, and all these Foster investigations—she did not realize it until now. Bernie was not shutting her out. *He was trying to protect her.* Because a call from Deb Coyle outside the Oval was a call from Bill, a call from Bernie from the counsel's office was a call from Hillary.

Linda had heard those very words, intimidating words, while serving in the counsel's office directed at others during all the Clinton investigations. She knew exactly what that meant. "I'm calling on behalf of the President of the United States ..." from the president's lawyers to "I'm calling on behalf of the First Lady of the United States, the First Lady wants you to know ..." from her former boss or Foster speaking for Hillary. No threats were necessary. The message was always crystal clear. *Are you going to go up against the leader of the free world and his wife, the co-president?*

We stared at each other in silence for what seemed like a long time, but probably wasn't. Not one word crossed our lips. It was not necessary. We both knew the implications as it set in.

The day after Foster's death marked the beginning of the end, and life at the White House changed forever. For several staffers, including Linda and her boss, Nussbaum, although they followed orders, their days serving in the Clinton administration were quickly coming to a close.

July 21, 1993, began what those on the Left described as a continuation of a political vendetta against the Clintons that lasts until today. For the Right, it began the cover-up. I guess Bill Clinton would say I was trying to get blood out of a turnip, but the truth was finally within my reach. Thank God I now had a new direction to follow. I was right where I needed to be.

# 6

# Inside Hillary's White House Counsel's Office

"For where envying and strife is,
there is confusion and every evil work."

**—James 3:16 (KJV)**

It was early morning on July 21, 1993, when Linda, with little sleep and in shock, drove to the White House. She parked, flashed the White House guards her coveted blue pass with a "W," which granted her unescorted access to the West Wing and the president, and was promptly cleared in. Taking the main elevator up to the second floor, she headed directly to her desk in Hillary's counsel's office, hoping against reality that last night's phone call was a nightmare, and Foster would be hard at work in his office. Her feet carried her quickly when she passed the rarely used freight elevator in the West Wing.

"It blew my mind," she said, when she walked inside. "There was not one guard, no Secret Service agents, no police tape, nothing." At minimum, one would have assumed that the Park Police would have sealed off Foster's office shortly after he was identified.

What Linda did not know that morning was White House officials ignored four separate law enforcement requests to seal Foster's office. [142]

More than ten hours had passed since the White House "officially" knew Foster was dead. According to a press release the White House received "the positive identification ... at approximately 9:55 p.m."[143] White House staffers Craig Livingston and counsel to the president Bill Kennedy, a long-time Arkansas friend and former Rose Law Firm lawyer, identified the body—not Foster's family.[144]

The timeline in the White House statement differs from evidence obtained by Starr which showed that according to the hospital logs where Foster's body was taken, Kennedy and Livingston "viewed the body near 10:30 p.m."[145]

Likewise, the White House's account differs from the Secret Service, who apparently were notified of Foster's death "at about 8:30 p.m."[146] A discrepancy also exists with George Stephanopoulos' notification timeline. According to his writings, he found out shortly before 9:30 p.m., and he called Web Hubbell to tell him: "Vince killed himself."[147]

The inconsistencies in the death notification were never explained, and the conspiracy beast continued to growl. Foster's wife, Lisa, did not learn of her husband's death until approximately 10:10 p.m.

Inside the counsel's office, Linda found Betsy Pond on the phone all alone. An anomaly, she said, and one of the rare times she had recalled Pond coming to work before she did. When Pond saw Linda she apparently jumped in front of her like a linebacker, almost ripping the phone out of the wall, and shrieked, "Bernie said don't go into Vince's office," then closed Foster's office door.

"If I was half asleep then, I wasn't again," Linda tensely recalled. "She scared me awake."

What was Pond shielding Linda from seeing inside Foster's office? An office she had been in a million times before. It didn't make sense. Was Linda exaggerating?

No, she insisted and stood up, "Let me show you," she said.

In a mock reenactment, Linda recreated the moment for me. "Okay, it was really weird. You be me," she said. "Stand here."

Leading me in front of a doorway, she guided me into her position.

"I'll be Betsy. Remember how small the counsel office is," Linda reminded me as she pointed out the approximate diameters of the cramped suite she had once shared with Hillary's lawyers.

I barely took half a step inside the doorway when Linda flew out in front of me, bouncing back and forth, in front of the door, blocking any hope of me taking another step. "See, there was no way I could pass by her," Linda said. "Weird, don't you think?"

Linda said she knew Foster's office could be a *crime scene*. There was no way she would have set foot inside his office, and possibly contaminate any evidence. "I was going to my desk like I did every morning," she insisted.

What Linda did not know at the time was Foster's office, a possible crime scene, had already been contaminated. At minimum her boss, Hillary's chief of staff, and the director of White House administration had already gone in and out of it. Secret Service officer Henry O'Neill, an eighteen-year veteran, testified seeing staffers "exiting Foster's office with documents," sometime after his 10:30 p.m. shift at the White House had started that night.[148]

Hillary would go on to defend her senior aides' questionable actions the evening of Foster's death when she wrote in her memoir, "Since Vince's office was never a crime scene, these actions were understandable, legal, and justifiable," curiously pronouncing that Foster's office was *not a crime scene* before the investigation into his shocking death had barely begun.[149]

Linda, unlike Hillary, was not the only staffer and non-lawyer who understood Foster's office could be *a crime scene*. Press Secretary Dee Dee Myers did too. She was in the chief of staff's office, when a White House aide came in and told her, "The maids were upstairs and they're about to go into or they did go into Vince's office. Don't you think we ought to preserve what was in his trash?" Myers agreed, "God. I mean we're not thinking like law enforcement experts here. This is the scene of a crime."[150]

Daily, cleaning crews vacuum and toss out the trash in the West Wing. With Foster's office unsealed, the crews innocently could have thwarted evidence-gathering opportunities. The White House later claimed to have retrieved what was apparently tossed out.

*This is the scene of a crime.*

When Pond escorted Linda to her chair that morning, "She told me how she had disarmed the alarm system, and gone inside Foster's office to search for a suicide note, while straightening up his papers."[151] Finding no note, she apparently called to tell Nussbaum. Linda gasped, "I couldn't believe Betsy did that and told her so. I thought she was nuts. Actually I yelled at her. 'How could you go in there? Vince is dead. Where are the police? Don't touch anything.'"

If what Linda remembered was accurate, there was no reason for Pond to search for a suicide note; especially if she had spoken to Nussbaum, because he had already been inside Foster's office the night of his untimely death, allegedly looking for a suicide note and said he had found nothing.[152]

Nussbaum and Pond shared a long work history

together. He had brought her to the White House to work with him and later he had felt "guilty" about it. According to a deposition (in another Clinton investigation, "Filegate") Nussbaum testified how Betsy Pond "was less able to withstand those pressures [in the counsel's office] and was burning out ... Linda Tripp was sort of tougher and better able to withstand those pressures."[153]

Ultimately, Pond left the White House. Author of *Monica's Story*, Andrew Morton wrote how, "Tripp told investigators that a fellow secretary had a drink problem."[154] It sounded catty and spiteful, but Linda insisted that was not her intention. Rather it was about how they dealt with stress and pressure differently. "Betsy was an alcoholic, who would come to work smelling like the bottom of a scotch bottle," she said. "Me? After Vince died, I ate nonstop."

———

Hillary claimed she had "craved information like oxygen," when she learned of Foster's death and "was frantic because she felt so far away and couldn't figure out what was going on."[155] However, her actions and the actions inside the counsel's office suggest otherwise.[156]

Phone records disclosed two years after Foster's death showed Hillary called the White House at least four times that night into the early morning, including calling her chief of staff, Maggie Williams. "Immediately after speaking with Mrs. Clinton, Ms. Williams proceeded to Mr. Foster's office." After searching Foster's office, Williams called Hillary in "Little Rock at 12:56 a.m. on July 21, 1993."[157]

Inside the counsel's office, Linda's boss, Nussbaum, looking exhausted and disheveled, as she recalled, rushed into the suite about twenty minutes after she had arrived. He went directly to his office, adjacent to Foster's, apparently greeting Linda and Pond with a door slam.

"There were no hellos, no sorrys, no words of shock and sadness from Bernie, just a swift vibrating door slam—that couldn't be misconstrued," Linda stated. "Then Hillary put her troops in motion."

Instantaneously, top-notch lawyers and White House aides, "temporarily lost their minds, and ran frantically amok," she recounted.

One by one, Bill Kennedy, Steve Neuwirth, Bruce Lindsey, Cliff Sloan, Web Hubbell, George Stephanopoulos, and various associate counsels, flew into Nussbaum's office, slamming the door behind them.

It was now after 10:00 a.m. when Park Police investigators, Chief Robert Langston and Major Robert Hines, arrived. Forbidden access into Foster's closed-door office, the investigators had no choice but to join the Clintons' lawyers in a closed-door session in Nussbaum's office.

Linda was stunned. It did not make sense—at least not yet.

The White House lawyers' meeting with the Park Police investigators lasted for approximately thirty minutes when the investigators were escorted out of the counsel's office. Meanwhile, FBI agents, relegated to observe instead of to investigate, sat waiting impatiently downstairs.

When the Clintons first took office, they had ushered in a more open and casual policy for West Wing staffers. Linda remembered how previously all the support staff enjoyed "unlimited access to Nussbaum and to all the offices." After Foster died, that changed, she asserted. Not only were investigators barred from Foster's office, but now the staffers were shut out too.

Nussbaum later testified Linda must have been mistaken about the stark closed door changes that she remembered had occurred in the counsel's office after Foster's death. "But it's hard to confuse a closed door to an open door," she maintained without a hint of malice. Instead, Linda appeared troubled that her former boss contradicted her testimony.

"Betsy and Deb felt the stark changes too, 'I don't understand. It's a siege mentality but who's the enemy?'" Linda recalled Gorham once commenting.

So what were the White House lawyers doing?

According to what Hillary wrote in her memoir, *Living History*, they were not planning Foster's funeral because the funeral had been co-coordinated by Webb Hubbell. "In one of our numerous calls, Bill told me how Webb was a pillar of strength and efficiency, taking charge of the funeral that would be held in Little Rock …"[158]

So what were the Clintons' lawyers doing in the counsel's office?

"The usual," Linda calmly replied. "They were working out their cohesive strategy with Hillary." *What they would tell America had happened.*

Meanwhile the counsel's office persisted in its lack of common sense, leaving the most obvious undone. Incredibly, Foster's office still remained unsealed.

Earlier, Linda had shut the main doors to the counsel's suite when other staffers began milling around, hovering, curious, "I'm sure you understand," she explained as she closed the doors, when finally Neuwirth popped his head out of Nussbaum's office, "Get a guard," he said to Linda. But she had already on her own initiative requested one and had called the Presidential Protective Division.[159] It was appalling.

As she sat in her chair she could not believe how Hillary's lawyers were acting, she could not believe that she would never see Foster again. Through tears, Linda gazed at his closed office door, her thoughts racing. *I can't believe you are dead, my dear friend. Why didn't you come to me? What was so bad? What were you afraid of—afraid we would find out ...*

"It was unbelievable. These lawyers were not stupid, particularly Bernie, who is brilliant," Linda recalled. "Had I not seen it myself, I would not have believed it either—that's why everything that happened is so shocking."

———

Rewind to inside Hillary's counsel's office, July 21, 1993.

Linda was frozen in her chair.

In between answering an assault of phone calls, she sat at her desk and cried. Reeling from shock and grief, she watched what she called "the activation of a chain of command" be set into motion where a treasured member had sat a few hours before. Now Foster's body lay cold in a morgue. Intern Tom Castleton, escorted by Hillary's chief of staff Maggie Williams (who Linda pointed out never made a move unless she cleared it first by Hillary) went in and out of Foster's office, slamming the door behind them each time.[160] Together they lugged out as many boxes as they could each carry.

Castleton later testified, "As he helped carry the files to the residence, Williams told him the president or First Lady had to review the contents of the boxes to determine what was in them."[161]

Meanwhile, like a baseball catcher with two gloves, Nussbaum fielded calls like a Hall of Fame pro, from Hillary, Susan Thomases (Hillary's close advisor and a member of the Whitewater defense team during the 1992 presidential campaign), and Williams (when Williams wasn't hauling out stuff from Foster's office).

But even the willing Nussbaum could not handle all their calls and needed Linda for backup.

"Hillary kept us very busy," Linda remembered with a chill. "We couldn't hang up fast enough before the phone rang again. Hillary was crisp, all business, with not a word of condolence. 'Get me Bernie now!' to 'I don't give a f—k who he is talking to. Get him now!'"

With Hillary wielding an iron hand from Arkansas, an "agitated, uppity" Nussbaum responded, following Hillary's orders, as he nervously ran his fingers up and down the back of his skull.

"'Yes, it's taken care of,' Nussbaum assured Hillary. 'Calm down. No, I've already spoken to Susan.'" Linda grimly detailed some of their conversations for me. "Hillary's demands were so loud I could hear them before Bernie shut his door again. 'Keep them the f—k out!' Hillary ordered referring to the investigators, 'They can't have access.'"

Linda shuddered as she remembered. "Hillary wasn't upset Vince was dead. She was angry." And it appeared Nussbaum caught the brunt of Hillary's wrath.

Considering Foster's office was the last place he was seen alive, I could not understand why Nussbaum denied giving investigators unrestricted access to Foster's office despite Hillary's demands. Checking the last place a person is seen alive is basic law enforcement 101. Didn't Bernie want to find out everything there was to know about Foster's death?

"I know," Linda agreed, "But nobody challenged Hillary. Not even Bernie. If that's what Hillary wanted—she got it."

Was Linda exaggerating?

Consider how one White House advisor described Hillary's menacing influence: "People were scared of [Hillary] because they knew she could chop off their testicles if she so chose. You did not cross Hillary."[162]

Hillary also approved President Bill Clinton's moves according to another White House aide: "The joint decision-making at the top was so overt that staff members called Hillary 'The Supreme Court.' Whenever Bill said, 'Let me think about it,' aides knew he intended to call Hillary."[163]

Was Linda embellishing her boss's response to Hillary's cold and calculated orders to keep investigators out of Foster's office?

Not likely considering that phone records the Senate Whitewater committee obtained during their investigation back Linda up. They show how two days after Foster's death, Hillary was still concerned about the investigators having access to Foster's office. The records show that [Susan] Thomases paged Nussbaum "after talking" with Hillary, Thomases "then called [Hillary] back."[164]

Neuwirth testified that "later that morning" Nussbaum had said that Hillary and Susan "were concerned about law enforcement officials having 'unfettered access' to Foster's office."[165]

But investigators rightfully grew impatient.

Meanwhile, the afternoon of July 21, Nussbaum had negotiated an agreement with the Park Police and the Department of Justice. Now it appeared that the investigators would be permitted the following day to "look for signs of a note or other evidence that [Foster] might have taken his own life." The "agreement" Nussbaum had negotiated stipulated that a "member of the counsel's office" would be present during the "limited" investigation of Foster's office.[166] Someone from the Department of Justice would also be present to monitor the investigators because of "executive privilege."[167]

Citing executive privilege, the "right of the president of the United States to withhold information from

Congress or the courts," during the Foster death investigation was highly unusual considering executive privilege typically is applicable only when national security, military, and diplomatic secrets are involved— as opposed to personally protecting the first family or any person.

While the concept of "executive privilege" does not appear in the U.S. Constitution, prior U.S. presidents, most notably President Richard Nixon, had invoked it before President Clinton did.

In the 1974 Supreme Court case United States v. Nixon, for instance, Watergate special prosecutor Archibald Cox had requested Oval office-taped conversations between President Nixon and his colleagues in relation to the June 1972 break-in at the Democratic National Committee at the Watergate office complex. At the time President Nixon had refused to comply with lawful subpoenas and provide any records. Instead he invoked executive privilege.[168]

However, the court ruled against him, stating that Nixon's "generalized need for confidentiality did not outweigh the public's larger interest in carrying out criminal prosecution." The Supreme Court decision said in part: "To read the Article II powers of the President as providing an absolute privilege as against a subpoena essential to enforcement of criminal statutes on no more than a generalized claim of the public interest in confidentiality of non-military and non-diplomatic discussions would upset the constitutional balance of a workable government and gravely impair the role of the courts under Article III."[169]

Moreover, the type of "limited investigation" the Clintons' counsel office had orchestrated of Foster's office was actually a *non-investigation* because it blocked agents from conducting a thorough evidence search that could have conclusively ruled out homicide in Foster's death or shed light on suicide.

It did not make sense—at least not yet.

Even if investigators roamed freely in Foster's office, the Clintons' attorney-client relationship would be protected because, as previously mentioned, "Somebody from the Justice Department [would be present] monitoring to preserve the executive privilege."[170]

Why would Hillary, whose protected files—what remained of them—care if the Park Police or FBI went into Foster's office or for that matter looked under his desk? Didn't she want to know everything there was to know about her friend's sudden death? What was Hillary afraid the investigators would see?

Linda kept describing to me how she had felt an overriding sense of urgency to "cover." It was not a sense she could fully explain or articulate but she repeatedly insisted it was very real. "The cover-up feeling began immediately and never stopped," she maintained. So the obvious question to ask then is: what was being covered up?

# 7

# Jeopardy

"Be not a witness against thy neighbor without cause;
and deceive not with thy lips."

**—Proverbs 24:28 (KJV)**

It was late morning, July 21, when President Clinton stopped by the counsel's office for what Linda had assumed was a condolence call, except no words of condolence crossed his lips. How a person reacts during a tragedy naturally affects people differently. Grief is unique and apparently President Clinton was not an exception.

Linda was still shell-shocked, fighting off morbid thoughts and anguished visuals of Foster alone with blood pouring out of his head in a gruesome puddle, making her want to throw up, while she somberly introduced a "dry-eyed" President Clinton to the counsel's office support staff, who had yet to personally meet him (Linda had previously served directly for the president at the Oval office). When Linda and President Clinton briefly stopped at her desk to wait for Nussbaum, the president broke into an awkward trivia-like chatter, reminiscent of a one-sided episode of the game show *Jeopardy*.

"It was weird," Linda recalled. "President Clinton kept asking me questions, while he pointed towards a poster of a walled city that hung on the wall above her desk. Ironically, next to that poster hung a personal memento she had preserved in a simple frame. It was The Code of Ethics for Government, something Linda had kept for years, cherished, and knew by heart, "1. Put loyalty to the highest moral principles and to country above loyalty to Government persons, party or department ..." it reads in part.[171]

"And the president asked me if I could name the other walled cities, like a history test," Linda elaborated, flicking her head at the wacky memory. "It was vintage Clinton. He kept quizzing and answering his own questions, showcasing his encyclopedia memory, his steel trap recollection that seemed to escape him only when he was under oath. It seemed so peculiar, so out of place. Didn't mention Vince."

Finally an overwhelmed, grief-stricken, and jumpy Nussbaum interrupted Clinton's trivia showcasing with Linda. But right before President Clinton went off with her boss, Linda expressed her condolences, "I'm very sorry about Vince, Mr. President," she said. "He seemed taken aback, preoccupied, and he just said, 'Oh, ah, well, thank you,'" and turned on his heels to face Nussbaum. Then President Clinton hurriedly followed him into Foster's office and shut the door.

"Bernie was acting completely out of character to what I'd known before," Linda recapped again, almost apologizing for her boss's bizarre actions. "I know it sounds crazy," she said, "but I couldn't shake the feeling that President Clinton was there to make sure Bernie had done everything he was ordered to do."

If Linda's instinct was right, what was President Clinton checking to see that Nussbaum and Hillary's aides had done for him and Hillary inside Foster's office?

———

At noon that day, at President Clinton's request, a staff meeting was convened in the Old Executive Office Building (OEOB) Theater in Room 450, across the street from the White House to remember Foster. Inside the theater it was standing room only, stacked with shocked and forlorn staffers. Linda sat in the first row with Pond and Gorham among the sea of sadness, confusion, and disbelief that swept over the audience. The counsel's office was vacant apart from the guards posted outside under Craig Livingston's direction.

Three men took turns speaking at the podium to remember Foster, their friend and colleague. Chief of Staff Mack McLarty "gave a polished speech" Linda remembered. "Grief stricken and in tears, Bernie poignantly eulogized Vince from his recent perspective, working with a colleague who became a friend. He injected a little humor, and reminisced, how Vince interviewed him, and really was the counsel to the president."

Nussbaum had also vividly described what he said was the last time he had seen Foster alive. Sitting in his office, he had been flipping between TV news coverage that reported on Judge Louis Freeh's nomination to head the FBI, and the U.S. Senate confirmation hearings with Judge Ruth Bader Ginsburg's opening statement for her appointment to the Supreme Court that occurred as well that day.

"And I said to my partner, 'Vince,' I said, 'Hey, Vince, not a bad day.' I said, 'We hit two home runs. Not home runs for you, Vince, or even for the president; really home runs for the country. So I think we're doing our job, and I think we're doing it well.'"[172]

Following Nussbaum, President Clinton spoke at the podium.

"I'll never forget it," Linda recollected. "Clinton probably gave the most compelling speech I ever heard, but it was devoid of any emotion."

President Clinton said in part: "Forty-two years ago, when I met Mr. McLarty in kindergarten, I lived with my grandparents in a modest little house around the corner from Vince Foster's nice, big, white brick house ...

"Yesterday, last night, when I finished the *Larry King Show,* and I was told what happened, I was just thinking in my mind of when we were young, sitting on the ground in the back yard, throwing knives onto the ground and seeing if we were adroit enough to make them stick.

"When I started my career in Arkansas politics, he was there to help me. When I decided to run for attorney general, he was the first lawyer in Little Rock I talked to about supporting me. When the Rose Law Firm hired Hillary after I moved to Little Rock, Vince Foster and Webb Hubbell became her closest friends ... *No one can ever know why this happened.* Even if you had a whole set of objective reasons, that wouldn't be why it happened, because you could get a different, bigger, more burdensome set of objective reasons that are on someone else even in this room. *So what happened was a mystery about something inside of him. I hope all of you will always understand that* [emphasis mine]."

At a press briefing that day, President Clinton reiterated how "there is no way to know why these things happen." Foster's suicide would always remain a mystery, and it "was a mystery about something inside him." [173]

But Foster was dead for less than twenty-four hours. How could President Clinton be so sure we would never know why? How could he be so sure Foster had committed suicide?

"The White House ensured we'd never know," Linda repeated. "When President Clinton said that, he knew that part was true."

After the assembly disbanded, a devastated, crying Linda spoke to senior presidential aide Bruce Lindsey. Knowing that everybody would jockey to fly to Arkansas on Air Force One, she told him how she needed to be at the funeral, she needed to see Foster put to rest, and asked him if he knew what Foster's funeral arrangements were so she could call the travel office to arrange to be there.

Later that day, Linda was surprised and relieved when she saw her name on the July 23 flight manifesto for Air Force One—destination Little Rock, Arkansas.

# 8

# You Are Not Going

# To Get Much

"Your sin prompts your mouth;
you adopt the tongue of the crafty."

—Job 15:5 (NIV)

It was late on July 21 when a counsel's office roundtable was assembled for the staffers. Called a meeting on "comportment and interrogation," the briefing prepared them for when the Park Police investigators would come to question each of them. It also addressed how their personal conduct and demeanor should be presented with law enforcement. Pond, Gorham, and Linda took their places across from Nussbaum, Sloan, and Neuwirth. Uncharacteristically, Nussbaum took a back seat, initially allowing his subordinate lawyers to give directions.

Once again the staffers were told how Vince was found in Fort Marcy Park, dead from suicide, and they would never know what really happened, even though the investigation had barely begun.

Having never taken instruction from anyone except Nussbaum before, Linda could not understand why the entire dynamic changed. She was feeling somewhat comfortable until Nussbaum spoke up and said, "The police are coming to question each of us. You are to be truthful and answer their questions, but no speculations. Each of you will be accompanied by one of us."

Accompanied? Why? Linda had nothing to hide. Her single priority was to help investigators find out everything there was to know about Foster's death. A cloak of intimidation shrouded her. A nagging feeling that something was wrong hit her with a vengeance because she knew that when Nussbaum spoke, he was conveying Hillary's orders. Others reportedly verify Linda's recall of Hillary's calling-the-shots, behind-the-scenes role.

"In fact, playing the role of 'hidden hand' is one [Hillary] enjoys. She was extremely Machiavellian, a master of doing things that could not be traced back to her," recalled one close colleague. "She would say, 'Do this, but don't leave any fingerprints.'"[174]

Next, Nussbaum slipped into his fast-talking lawyer mode. Like a cobra, he was ready to strike out any concerns the staffers had about being accompanied by a counsel office lawyer when they met with the Park Police with quick answers like, "I wouldn't send anyone into interviews conducted by law enforcement without counsel."

Linda took that to mean the usual; the Clintons were, as always, keeping tabs. Something was very wrong. Nussbaum persisted with what Linda believed to be Hillary's script to coach the staffers. It was the classic defense the Clintons had used to combat all the other investigations. It went like this: "Nothing here. The investigators are on a political witch hunt. So make it short and sweet and get out. They're trying to take down the president. Don't speculate."

Except Foster was found dead less than twenty-four hours earlier, perhaps the investigators just wanted to do their jobs and investigate Foster's death—not play politics with the Clintons.

"It was awful, but I was afraid for my job," Linda described to me as she relived that time with tears welling in her eyes. "I've always respected law enforcement, and here I am in the White House ordered to consider all law enforcement as the enemy. Ordered not to speculate or offer information that could help them find out what had happened to him. Vince's death became all about them, and protecting themselves. I couldn't understand why they wouldn't do everything possible to find out why Vince died, especially Bernie— they were so close."

The counsel's office lawyers were the Clintons' lawyers, who were tasked to look out for *their* best interests, and Linda would have preferred having *her own* counsel—if counsel was even necessary. It was unnerving. The White House demands appeared to be reasonable if there was a crime but *not reasonable* if they truly wanted to get to the bottom of why their cherished friend and colleague was suddenly, mysteriously found dead with a bullet in his head in a park.

Naturally, the staffers were advised to get lawyers, White House-appointed ones, *after* they went on the record with investigators accompanied by White House counsel. Now the staffers would be forever boxed in by the Clinton White House's version of events.

This strategy is also known as the Clintons' "joint defense" tactic; a tactic which became public knowledge during the Clinton-Lewinsky investigation, called the *joint defense agreement* strategy. Unbeknownst to most Americans, the joint defense tactic was successfully used to benefit and protect the Clintons during all the investigations. It's where witnesses may not communicate with one another; lawyers, however, may legally share information among others lawyers ensuring that the White House was always informed on who said what.[175]

With dread, Linda knew the investigators were not going to get much the next day when she met them accompanied by an associate White House counsel. Uncomfortable and intimidated, she wrestled with her conscience and lost.

*Why won't the Clintons let us speculate, or offer information which might be helpful? Don't they want to know what happened to Vince?*

With a sick sense of déjà-vu, she drew upon the rationalization skills she had mastered during Travelgate, when she watched Billy Dale, a man she admired and respected, be falsely indicted on trumped up embezzle-ment charges by the Clinton White House.[176] As she later testified, "And I will never forgive myself for not warning [the travel office staff] when I saw what was being done to them. But I didn't. I chose to be *loyal to the Office of the Counsel to the President* [italics mine] for whom I worked and made a decision not to give them fair warning about what was going to happen to them."[177]

It was like dancing with the devil. Her justification loop played like this: Serving at the White House was an honor and privilege. She wanted to stay, hoped to do good … her job, her pension, and her kids …

And now, all these years later, Linda had admitted to me that she was a coward during the Park Police interviews into Foster's death when she followed her intimidating orders. "I was afraid. I couldn't go against President Clinton and Hillary. We all were afraid," Linda justified and rationalized. "We all knew we were in deep trouble if we didn't stick to their version when we spoke to investigators. We were told what happened and what to say, and suddenly that became the so-called truth, but it was too soon for anybody to know exactly what had happened to Vince."

*Thou shalt not bear false witness.*

So instead of being forthcoming and entirely truthful with investigators or resigning in protest to defy the Clinton White House orders that would obstruct and skew the investigation into Foster's death, Linda played by the Clintons' rules. She compromised her long-held ethics, her Christian values by allowing her fear of the Clintons to preempt her fear of God and became something she wasn't when she surrendered her freedom to tell the truth for a paycheck. So she spoke with the investigators "narrowly and carefully" sticking with the Clinton version of events. The White House lawyers ensured the Clintons' cohesive strategy became the official record. Now they owned her. She hated it, and she ate nonstop afterwards, but she did it. As always, she said she had no choice.

"It felt wrong, really wrong. Nobody likes to have Hillary's henchmen breathing down their neck. None of us did. I was scared for my job. We all were. What would you do if you had the power of the White House breathing down your neck?"

Feeling trapped, Linda bristled, as she continuously justified herself. "The Park Police found my White House 'escort' as disconcerting as I did," she said.[178]

Her escort, who she described as being "joined to her hip," assured their quizzical faces, "We're just here to make sure everything is recorded accurately."[179]

Sound farfetched and unethical? The Senate Whitewater Committee investigation confirmed Linda's recollection of events that day: "Members of the White House counsel's office participated in the Park Police interviews of White House staffers, not to protect the legal interests of the staffers but ... to report back to Mr. Nussbaum what was being said in the interviews."

Moreover, "the White House counsel's office coached the staffers about their testimony during a meeting on 'comportment and interrogation.' The Park Police left with the impression that their interviews had been rehearsed."[180]

The Committee's report continues, "because the White House lawyers were present, '[t]he atmosphere of those interviews made it impossible to establish any kind of relationship with the people being interviewed.' The lawyers created an 'intimidating situation' and therefore the interviews were not very productive."

According to Park Police Detective Peter Markland: "It was my belief that the staff members that we were interviewing had been briefed beforehand and would say no more than what they were told they should tell us ... Everyone I interviewed on this day up there I felt had been talked to by Mr. Nussbaum or his staff and knew exactly what they were going to say, nothing more, nothing less. And that was it. They all came off very rehearsed."[181]

Detective Markland's assessment was right. The staffers were coached, their interviews were scripted. The truth was damned.

Please remove your ideological glasses here, and ask yourself if the Clintons are above the law? The counsel's office's misconduct during the Foster investigation was not an isolated incident; rather it was typical. Consider President Clinton's conduct with investigators during the events that led to his impeachment.

In 2001, OIC special prosecutor Robert Ray, in a last-minute deal with President Clinton found Bill Clinton, "knowingly gave evasive and misleading answers to questions ... and that his conduct was prejudicial to the administration of justice. He has acknowledged [after he was caught lying because of forensics—semen on a dress] that some of his answers were false."[182]

*I'm calling on behalf of the president ... I'm calling on behalf of the First Lady ...*

The fish rots from the head down. One cannot serve under corrupt leadership and not become corrupt or compromised themselves. I could not help but wonder whether Linda, during her interview with the Park Police, had felt like Foster might have felt before he died—trapped by the Clintons—when he had said in an interview with *Time Magazine* shortly before his death, *"Before we came here we thought of ourselves as good people."*[183] So did Linda.

The cover-up air inside the Clinton White House resumed.

———

Dumbstruck, Linda's jaw hit the floor.

It was July 22, 1993, the day investigators were permitted *partial* access to Foster's office—or so they had mistakenly thought.

Linda did not know about the series of early morning phone calls that began at 7:44 a.m. when Williams called Hillary in Arkansas. Nor did Linda know about Hillary's call to Thomases or that Thomases, minutes after hanging up with Hillary, paged Nussbaum. Thomasas spoke with Nussbaum twice that morning.[184]

What Linda did know as she sat at her desk was at approximately 10:00 a.m., Nussbaum had a last-minute change for the investigators: he "alone would review the documents" in Foster's office.[185] That change meant that two justice department attorneys, agents from the FBI, the Park Police, and Secret Service, were now permitted *to watch* Nussbaum in Foster's office with White House counsel Clifford Sloan and Steven Neuwirth.[186]

"It was unbearable," Linda gasped, reliving how she viewed in appalled amazement the boss she admired scold and patronize the investigators. At one point Sloan accused an investigator of peeking at a document when he stood up to stretch.[187] The investigators were permitted to remain *in only one area* of Foster's office.[188]

Standing behind Foster's desk, Nussbaum made three piles of papers while the investigators "observed." Linda described how her boss would hold up a page at a time and sometimes cite "executive privilege." Other times he would open Foster's desk drawer and taunt law enforcement, by saying, "See?! —Nothing."

"There was always a sense in this White House that you were either with them or against them," Linda reiterated. "But Bernie was acting outrageous. The investigators weren't out to get the Clintons. They were trying to find out what happened to Vince."

Does Linda's recollection of Nussbaum's conduct in Foster's office sound unbelievable? Perhaps, except the investigators confirmed her recollection. They complained how "dissatisfied" they were with Nussbaum's "cursory review of documents" in "Foster's office."[189]

As the *New York Times* reported, "Mr. Nussbaum kept law-enforcement officials at arm's-length in Mr. Foster's office while he sat at Mr. Foster's desk and reviewed the documents himself, one by one, deciding which could be turned over to the investigators. In one instance ... Mr. Nussbaum *would not let law enforcement officials in the room* even to see a newspaper clipping found in Mr. Foster's files, asserting it was shielded by executive privilege (emphasis mine)."[190]

In the Clintons' upside-down world of cooperation, the investigators from the Park Police, the Justice Department, and the FBI left Foster's office empty handed.

Clinton-appointed Deputy Attorney General Phillip Heymann was so incensed when he learned about the non-investigation that he confronted Nussbaum demanding to know if he were "hiding something? Is there some terrible secret here that you are hiding?"[191]

The Senate Whitewater Committee called it a "sham." The Committee found that the counsel's office, government lawyers, "who were supposed to protect public interest in a proper investigation and faithful execution of the laws, instead interfered and obstructed various federal investigations."

"Unquestionably, the Department of Justice and Park Police were authorized to conduct this investigation, and White House officials owed them a duty to cooperate. Instead, law enforcement officials were confronted at every turn with concerted efforts to deny them access to evidence in Mr. Foster's office." [192]

The committee concluded: "The actions of these senior White House officials constitute a highly improper pattern of deliberate misconduct," or as it would be called for everyday Americans, obstruction of justice.[193]

Was Nussbaum a willing participant or the ring-leader in obstructing investigators in the counsel's office, or was he following orders?

"No," Linda promptly defended her boss. "Bernie was following Hillary's orders. Nobody challenged the Clintons, not me, low on the totem pole, all the way to senior staff, including their lawyers. We all knew if we challenged them there would be hell to pay. Bernie was no different. You are challenging the leader of the free world and his wife, the co-president."

Press Secretary Myers recalled the danger of standing up to Hillary, during Whitewater, for instance, when Stephanopoulos challenged Hillary and regretted it, "Everyone just sat there and let George take the beating. Mrs. Clinton got really angry. She attacked George, which everyone knew was coming, which is why I guess nobody was willing to ride in there to the rescue ... Anybody that stood up" to Hillary and "tried to say this was a bad idea" was "smashed down." Hillary "belittled them, very personally." Hillary likes to dig in. "She wants to fight."[194]

Why would a first-rate lawyer risk his reputation and career by following Hillary's orders? Wouldn't Nussbaum want to know everything about Foster's death there was to know and cooperate with investigators? Dare I ask—what were Nussbaum and Hillary afraid that the investigators might see inside Foster's office?

But that's what happened. Less than a year after Foster's death, on March 5, 1994, Nussbaum resigned, publically humiliated, disgraced; a once noble and respected career tarnished because of his service in the Clinton White House. "Bernie resigned at a time when there were questions about the investigation of Vince Foster's suicide," said Special Counsel Jane Sherburne, who was brought in after he left. "There was a perception that [Foster and Whitewater] issues had been mishandled ... that they needed someone to come in who would restore some confidence, that there was a real grown-up in there."[195]

Although Nussbaum was disposable in the "ends justify the means" service to protect the Clintons, as of this writing, he maintains he did nothing wrong during the Foster death investigation—but what else could he say? *I go down, you go down.*

Two years after Foster's death, during the congressional Whitewater hearings, emails became public that preserved Linda's shock and dismay at what was occurring in Hillary's counsel's office after Foster died. In one email Linda referred to Nussbaum and two other White House lawyers as "the three stooges." In another, she complained about a three-day delay in looking into an important piece of evidence.

"Christ. And we're the support staff?" she wrote.[196]

Justice was turned back, and righteousness stood afar off; for truth had fallen in the street, and equity could not enter (Isaiah 59:14 NKJV).

# 9

# Plastic Flowers

"I will make mere youths their officials;
children will rule over them."

**—Isaiah 3:4 (NIV)**

On July 23, 1993, Foster was laid to rest in Hope,
Arkansas, the place of his birth. Linda en route to his
funeral looked out from a window on Air Force One,
the president's flying palace, and watched the runway in
Little Rock loom closer.

"Fasten your seatbelt," warned the pilot when
Pond, who was sitting next to Linda, passed her empty
cocktail glass over. Linda grabbed it and dumped it with
her empty candy bar wrappers into the trash. When the
cabin door opened, scorching, hot, Arkansas summer air
enveloped them.

President Clinton and his aides hit the limo as "we
loaded into the buses to escape the 103-degree heat,"
she remembered.

By 11:00 a.m., President Clinton, friends,
colleagues and families, were gathered at St. Andrew's
Roman Catholic Cathedral to say their final goodbyes.[197]
Foster's body had been flown in on a Department of
Defense plane to Arkansas the day before, accompanied
by Webb Hubbell. Hillary and her aides flew in on her
plane and met up with the group at the church.[198]

"Hillary was distant and cold. Bill was his usual self
with his funeral face," Linda detailed. "You know, the

one that you see on TV, except this was his friend who died, not a performance to win votes."

Inside the packed church it was "unbelievable," subdivided by level of importance. Linda sat in the balcony with Pond and looked down to see Foster's flag-draped coffin below.

"I know this may sound weird, and I don't want to sound nitpicky, but this sense of unreality overcame me," Linda described as she took in a deep breath, choosing her words carefully. "One by one, friends took turns speaking of their dearly departed friend, Vince …," she said. "It's hard to explain, but it was like—bury a friend and while we're here, how ya doing?"

Linda's vivid memories of Foster's funeral sounded so deeply unsettling to me that I was not sure what to make of them. Some of the words she used to describe it were: "tacky," "crass," and "plastic." Then, in October 2002, I saw exactly what Linda meant when the same words she used to describe what should have been Foster's solemn funeral were used to describe another memorial service the Clintons attended for Minnesota Senator Paul Wellstone.

In a tragic plane crash, Wellstone, his wife, and daughter were killed. At the time, it was reported how "several Republican grievers all but fainted at the sight of how tacky the proceedings were getting to be."[199] Critics accused Democrats of playing politics by turning Wellstone's memorial service into a "pep rally."[200]

After Foster's service was over, the church emptied out and a 40-car funeral procession formed behind Foster's casket, headed for Memory Garden Cemetery in Hope, his birthplace, and his final resting place where his mother still lived.

While Linda was married to Bruce M. Tripp, a career Army officer and a battalion commander, at different times during their twenty-year marriage they had lived in the South, including in Georgia and North Carolina, but *this* south, Arkansas, was unlike any she had known before. While she served in the White House, she had heard the whispers about "the Clintons' Arkansas—that's how they do business ..." but she never quite understood it until she saw it with her own eyes.

"It was hopeless," she said. "It became quickly apparent that if you had to live in Arkansas, you didn't want to be a have-not. The only way to survive was as one of them. No matter what the cost. I believe that's what Vince did—at a huge cost."

Weeks before his death, at a commencement address, on May 8, 1993, Foster told a graduating law class of his alma mater: "The reputation you develop for intellectual and ethical integrity will be your greatest asset or your worst enemy ... I cannot make this point to you too strongly: You will be judged by your judgment ... There is no victory, no advantage, no fee, no favor which is worth even a blemish on your reputation for intellect and integrity. Nothing travels faster than an accusation that another lawyer's word is no good ... Dents to [your] reputation are irreparable ... If you find yourself getting burned out or unfulfilled, unappreciated ... have the courage to make a change."[201]

Is that what Foster did?

Consider what lay ahead for some of the Clintons' friends and associates. After Foster's funeral, indictments slammed down and deals were cut.

On September 23, 1993, for example, President of Capital Management Services David Hale, after his office was raided by the FBI, was indicted by an Arkansas federal grand jury in connection with Hillary and Bill Clinton's Whitewater investigations.[202] In December 1994, Webb Hubbell was convicted of defrauding the Rose Law Firm, where Hillary and Foster worked closely together with him. (During the Senate Whitewater Committee investigation, Hubbell "provided inaccurate and incomplete testimony to the Committee in order to conceal Mrs. Clinton's pivotal role in the decisions surrounding the handling of Mr. Foster's documents following his death.")[203] Susan McDougal and her now deceased husband, James B. McDougal, the Clintons' partners in Whitewater, were convicted and imprisoned for their participation in the fraudulent bank loan scheme that began the Whitewater investigation. [204] (Susan McDougal later received a presidential pardon from Bill Clinton.)[205]

It was Foster who was tasked with making the argument defending Hillary's dubious status as a de facto federal official, an un-elected leader, to validate the secret hearings she insisted be held for HillaryCare, her health-care task force (what later became ObamaCare).[206]

Also looming in the background which may have tormented Foster was what became known as the tainted blood scandal that garnered little U.S. media coverage despite American's right to know about it before they voted in the 1992 presidential contest. Under then Governor Bill Clinton's watch Arkansas prisons sold HIV and hepatitis infected blood to countries including Canada, the UK and Scotland that claimed the lives of tens of thousands of people, and so forth. Naturally, the tainted blood story never made it into either Bill or Hillary Clinton's books.[207]

At last count, during the Clinton years and investigations, "one hundred and twenty-two congressional witnesses invoked their Fifth Amendment right against self-incrimination, or fled the country to avoid testifying or as was the case with foreign witnesses, they refused to be interviewed."[208]

After the bus ride, then standing by Foster's gravesite and final resting place, that surreal element Linda described to me had revisited her, "It was all plastic," she said. "Plastic funeral, plastic words. There were even plastic flowers on Vince's casket."

After Foster's casket was lowered into the ground, Hillary with her aides and President Clinton with his aides, "glommed around or near Foster's family," while Linda hung back from the group. Her feet were swollen and killing her so she took off her black high heel shoes. A Christian (as I am), she described to me how she looked up to the sky searching for answers, guidance.

After making the sign of the cross, she held her head down in a silent prayer: "God the Father, God the Son, God the Holy Ghost, please, God, bless Vince's soul, he's a good man. I know you know that. Please take him home to you. Please put a healing hand on Lisa and the children, and heal their breaking hearts and bless them with all the happiness Vince would want for them. Please, please, God, help me understand, and let me be guided in your truth and show me the way to make sure this never happens again. May we all find peace in your glory. Amen—and if Vince did commit suicide, please forgive him," she prayed hard.

En route back to the airport with the president and Hillary in front and the staffers and press corps following behind in buses to return to Washington, Linda remembered how the procession made a "watermelon stop" first before leaving Arkansas.

President Clinton confirmed Linda's peculiar watermelon memory.

As he wrote in his memoir, *My Life*, "… the watermelon crop had begun to come in. Before I left town, I stopped at Carter Russell's place and sampled both the red- and yellow-meated ones. Then I discussed the finer points of Hope's main product with the traveling press, who knew I needed a respite from the pain and were uncommonly kind to me that day ...."[209]

After the watermelon stop, on the airport tarmac, Linda would have normally "clawed" her way onto Air Force One to fly home. "It's an experience like none other," she said. As Stephanopoulos once described it, "To climb [Air Force One's] back steps was to enter a world even more rarefied than the White House itself. Inside the huge cabin are all the comforts of home and office combined; couches flanked by bowls of fresh fruit, and candy in the corridors; a conference room with two TVs in the wall and a library of first-run movies; offices with computers, fax machines, copies, and phones; a full kitchen crew serving hot meals and cold drinks around the clock. Up front, the president has a one-bedroom apartment with the office, full bath, and king-sized bed."[210]

But not that day after Foster's tacky, plastic funeral; instead Linda relinquished her coveted Air Force One seat because no creature comforts could appease her or calm her sorrow and turmoil. All she knew at that moment was she did not want to be around "them" any longer. So with Pond, who offered to join her, together they boarded Hillary's plane back to Washington, since Hillary had joined President Clinton on Air Force One.

The next day, "Steve was told to pack Vince's items up," Linda recalled with disgust. Officially, it was a "files and material inventory." And he did, with Foster's door slammed shut behind him—now standard practice in Hillary's counsel's office. [211]

# 10

# **Damage Control**

"A true witness delivereth souls:
but a deceitful witness speaketh lies."

**— Proverbs 14:25 (KJV)**

The following Monday, for the first time in days, Linda was asked to stay late at work. She was surprised because ever since Foster's death she had been on the other side of the closed door.

Counsel Cliff Sloan allegedly asked Linda to get a typewriter. Amazed by his request, she told me how she had glanced at the bank of computers, then at the floor where the cables were intertwined, and thought he must have been joking.

"Where was I going to get a typewriter?" Linda wondered. "But he kept insisting he wanted one."[212] She did not find a typewriter for him.

Sloan testified to the best of his recollection, his urgent typewriter request that Linda testified to escaped his memory. So who is telling the truth, and why does it matter? No one can know conclusively because as the Senate Whitewater investigations confirmed, Congress "faced numerous instances where witnesses provided inconsistent or contradictory testimony, and even more often … provided a rote response of 'I don't recall' or 'I have no specific recollection or knowledge' relating to crucial facts."[213]

What we do know is that on July 26, six days after

Foster's death, and Linda's alleged typewriter request from Sloan, what was described as a "suicide note" or a "note to himself that indicated a troubled state of mind" appeared in Foster's office.

Linda was working at her desk when Neuwirth who was packing up Foster's belongings, poked his head of out of Foster's office, and said to her, "Get Bernie—now," Linda recalled.[214]

Minutes after his demand, Hillary joined Nussbaum and Neuwirth, and closed the door to Foster's office.[215] We later learned the group was apparently trying to reconstruct an unsigned and undated note like a jigsaw puzzle on what had been a single sheet of yellow legal-size paper. The "note" had allegedly been torn into twenty-seven pieces and was found at the bottom of Foster's briefcase—the same brief case investigators recalled Nussbaum had inspected earlier without finding the note.[216]

Finally, the lawyers alerted the already suspicious office when the support staff was told, "There's a note."[217]

Finding the alleged suicide note was remarkable six days after Foster's death considering how a parade of Hillary's closest aides evidently missed finding it earlier. The investigators could not be blamed or held accountable for not finding the note because they were not permitted access to Foster's office to search for one.

"Hillary directed Chief of Staff McLarty and all the other aides not to tell the president about the note," Linda recalled, until a coherent position was developed.[218]

Upon hearing about the note, for Linda, her first instinct was to pick up the phone and notify somebody, the Park Police, Janet Reno, anybody, but Nussbaum, following Hillary's orders, said they were going to show it to Lisa Foster first—who was out of town, and the president, who was also unavailable.

"Can you imagine? We were told we had to wait until we reached the president. He's always reachable from the White House," Linda grumbled. "It's the president of the United States." [219]

But by then the counsel's office was in deep subterfuge. The staffers were warned investigators could come at any time. They were told to keep their mouths shut and mind their business. "Hillary never justified anything. Whatever she said goes," Linda said with misery. "But Bernie was uncomfortable as I was by Hillary's latest demand over the note."

Does Linda's recollection of Hillary's demands that everyone keep quiet about the note sound outrageous?

Consider what happened next. Lisa Foster and the Park Police were not shown the note until the following day; Lisa, in the afternoon and the Park Police at 8:00 p.m. As reported in the *New York Times*, "The White House waited for about 30 hours before giving federal investigators the scraps of a torn-up note found" in Foster's briefcase. "A senior White House official insisted that there was never any doubt that the note would be turned over, 'the only question was what was proper,' in terms of notifying the Foster family first and the president."

Days passed before Foster's alleged note became public.[220]

Three years after Foster's death a newly released memo written by a White House lawyer also confirmed Linda's recall. The memo quoted Chief of Staff Mack McLarty as saying that Hillary "was very upset and believed the matter required further thought and the president should not yet be told" about Foster's note. According to the document, Hillary "said they should have a *coherent position* and should have decided what to do before they told the president (emphasis mine)."[221]

Handwriting experts offered different opinions as to whether or not Foster wrote the note. The "FBI laboratory found one latent print on the note and determined that the print belonged to Bernie."[222] Nussbaum explained that his finger print was on the note because he had tried to piece it together.

Based on Nussbaum's explanation, is it reasonable to assume that had Foster written the note, and then shredded it into twenty-seven pieces, that the FBI laboratory might have found at least one fingerprint or, at least, a partial fingerprint that belonged to Foster? Yes, but the investigators did not find Foster's print on his so-called suicide note.[223]

It gets even stranger. Foster's "suicide" note did not mention how much he loved his family. He did not plead for their forgiveness for taking his life nor was there a whisper of any goodbyes; instead the note read more like a shopping list of items to exonerate the Clintons.

In the note Foster ostensibly vindicated of any misdeeds the Clintons, himself, White House staffers, and Hillary's Little Rock decorator Kaki Hockersmith, who was working with Hillary on the White House restorations. He accused the FBI, the *Wall Street Journal,* and the GOP ("the Grand Old Party," the Republicans), of lying, the press of a cover-up, and the White House usher's office of plotting to incur excessive costs during the White House renovations.

"The public will never believe the innocence of the Clintons and their loyal staff. I was not meant for the job or the spotlight of public life in Washington," Foster allegedly wrote. "Here ruining people is considered sport."[224]

Text of Foster's alleged suicide note:

*I made mistakes from ignorance, inexperience and overwork.*

*I did not knowingly violate any law or standard of conduct.*

*No one in the White House, to my knowledge, violated any law or standard of conduct, including any action in the travel office. There was no intent to benefit any individual or specific group.*

*The FBI lied in their report to the AG (Attorney General).*

*The press is covering up the illegal benefits they received from the travel office.*

*The GOP has lied and misrepresented its knowledge and role and covered up a prior investigation.*

*The Ushers office plotted to have excessive costs incurred taking advantage of Kaki [Kaki Hockersmith, the Clinton's decorator from Little Rock] and HRC [Hillary Rodham Clinton].*

*The public will never believe the innocence of the Clintons and their loyal staff.*

*The WSJ [Wall Street Journal] editors lie without consequence.*

*I was not meant for the job or the spotlight of public life in Washington. Here ruining people is considered sport.*

It was damage control time again at the Clinton White House because on July 21, a day after Foster's death, the White House initially announced, "There was no note."[225]

But then, as murder allegations swirled, and the conspiracy theories multiplied, on August 10, 1993, over two weeks later, Press Secretary Gearan faced the skeptical press to talk about "the note."

"I will not attempt to characterize what Mr. Foster might have meant by certain phrases or sentences," Gearan said. "It would not only be inappropriate, but it is certainly beyond anyone's capacity to interpret many of the words that [Foster] wrote here."

Hillary described the note in her memoir as "it was not so much a suicide note as a cry from the heart, an accounting of the things that were tearing his soul."[226]

Linda did not buy it. "It was a sick joke. Vince would never write a note like that," and described it as a "to-do-list of lies."

As she testified during the Clinton-Lewinsky investigations, "None of the behavior following Vince Foster's suicide computed to just people mourning Mr. Foster. It was far more ominous than that and it was extremely questionable behavior on the parts of those who were immediately involved in the aftermath of his death."[227]

# 11

# The Confession
# and the Case

"Your own mouth condemns you, and not I;
yes, your own lips testify against you."

**—Job 15:6 (NKJV)**

**W**hen the explosive words came out of Linda's mouth, unsolicited, about seven months after we first met, they were simultaneously heavy and light.

"You know," Linda nonchalantly said to me, one sunny afternoon, when we were seated in her living room in Middleburg, Virginia. "I think I could have been mistaken about the last time I saw Vince."

*What!?* She took me by surprise. My head exploded. *Mistaken!?*

Five government investigations had concluded Vince Foster committed suicide in Fort Marcy Park. He was depressed. Case closed. It was supposedly the end of the story. Linda, who had testified repeatedly in the Foster investigations, had never once breathed a word about any possible "mistake" she might have made. *Now you are mistaken?! Mistaken about what?*

Veteran law enforcement detectives agree that "countless cold cases have been solved years after a crime when a person's conscience forces the truth out."[228]

Was that what was happening here? Was Linda's conscience speaking, was it bearing witness? Conscience: "The awareness of a moral or ethical aspect of one's conduct together with the urge to prefer right over wrong."[229] I was inclined to believe that Linda preferred the truth over lies and right over wrong. Granted, I knew that could be temporarily suspended, muted by rationalizations, but for the most part ...

Then the memory of her confession was seared into my brain. With one arm dangling atop the backrest of the chair she sat on, Linda casually spun around and faced me directly. My eyes popped up from the stack of papers I was reading. My undivided attention was hers. Our eyes locked.

Then she said, "I can't say for sure that Vince didn't have his briefcase with him when he left the office."

Linda's revelation nearly knocked me sideways. My head must have swung in a double-take snap.

For a brief moment it was as though the sun shined in, for two reasons; firstly, because Linda had never ever admitted she could have been mistaken about anything before, without bombarding me with tortured rationales, justifying why she really was not wrong or why she didn't have a choice because she was following orders from the Clinton White House and was afraid she would lose her job—or worse if she didn't. And secondly, *Foster's briefcase, his briefcase! Foster had it with him—so what? Wait, what does this mean?*

I clung onto the diminishing breath that escaped my body. I choked out a pathetic, "What?"

"What I meant to say is," Linda stipulated, clearing her throat. "Is I couldn't testify today under oath and say for sure Vince wasn't carrying his briefcase when he left the office that day."

A calm rushed over me. A calm that accompanies truth and knowledge, and then it vanished. Meanwhile, Linda looked peaceful, relieved even, as my brain went bonkers. All the newspaper clippings, the books, the Park Police/Fiske/Starr/Clinger/Senate reports, I had studied and pored through. Like a bionic strobe light, pages of information flashed in my brain. *Who cares about Foster's briefcase? Dear God, why should I care?* Why was Linda's spontaneous revelation important?

Hey, wait a minute ... then ... as the memory of Linda's detailed Park Police interview, her description of the Clintons' cohesive strategy tactic, and the coaching settled sharply into focus: *"In every investigation we were told exactly what happened and what to say, and suddenly that became the so-called truth ..."*

I contemplated saying something profound; something adamant, bordering on accusatory even. Instead, I bit my tongue. *Let's see what Linda says next.* We sat through a short silence.

In an interview with the Park Police, two days after Foster's death, the investigators wrote: "Ms. Tripp makes it a habit to notice what the staff members are taking with them when they leave the office in order to determine ... how long she may expect them to be away from the office. Ms. Tripp was absolutely certain that Mr. Foster did not carry anything in the way of a briefcase, bag, umbrella, etc., out of the office."[230]

Three years later, Linda confirmed to OIC investigators that her detailed statement "accurately reflected her recollection."[231] *The investigators are trying to take down the president ... Don't speculate... Don't offer information ...*

"But then ..." I squeaked.

"I told you, we were told what to say—" Linda fired back, cutting me off, catching herself, followed by a non-apologetic backtrack. "Look, Tom thought Vince had his briefcase with him, so I, I, I must be mistaken."[232] *Mistaken?!*

In an instant, the heavy burden of towing the Clinton White House line appeared to have soared off of her, when a blink later, it spiked back down to earth, attached with her cover story.

Next the "Clintonese" (a term Linda used to describe doublespeak or memory lapses that occur when Clinton White House staffers are testifying) she insisted she despised, she recited to me, "I can't recall …" she stammered unrepentantly. "I can't be 100 percent sure that Vince didn't have his briefcase with him, that's all."

It was amazing, astonishing even—but what does her admission mean?

According to Starr's report, the initial Park Police interview two days after Foster's death with Betsy Pond and Tom Castleton did "not address" what Foster carried with him when he left his White House office.[233] Later in Office of Independent Counsel interviews, Pond initially could not recall what Foster carried (or did not carry), and then she remembered he had "his jacket swung over his shoulder." Castleton, however, recalled in an interview eight months later that Foster was "carrying a briefcase" when he left the office. He said it "looked very much like the old one that was in Foster's office on July 22."[234] Patsy Thomasson testified "she saw Foster's briefcase by the desk in his office on the night of July 20."[235]

*Then how did Foster's briefcase get inside of his office? The same briefcase—*

Why would the Park Police ask Linda about Foster's briefcase during the initial investigation, and not ask Pond and Castleton? It didn't make sense. Why did Linda break the sacred Clinton coaching rule to never offer investigators information because they were supposedly on a politically motivated fishing expedition to destroy the Clintons? [236]

When I asked her why, Linda threw the blame away from her, "It's the Squirrel Police. What do you expect? Look, I told you we were—" Her lips compressed, and then, a dark shadow flickered and passed over her eyes. The defensive Linda I knew was back.

Linda's vivid description of her Clinton White House escort hunted into my thoughts searching for prey, *"It was uncomfortable, intimidating. Nobody likes to have Hillary's henchmen breathing down their neck... The Park Police found my White House escort as disconcerting as I did. My 'escort,' assured their quizzical faces, 'We're just here to make sure everything is recorded accurately.'"*

"We knew if we challenged the Clintons there'd be hell to pay," Linda's habitually used excuse to justify her Clinton obedience during all the investigations replayed in my memory. "You're challenging the leader of the free world, and his wife, the co-president." *My job, my pension, my kids...*

Starr concluded: "Based on careful consideration ... the conclusions *significantly supported* are [emphasis mine]: (a) Mr. Foster's black briefcase remained in his office when he left on July 20; and (b) neither it nor another briefcase was in his car at Fort Marcy Park."[237]

Starr put his faith in Linda's detailed statement overruling Castleton's recollection. A statement she had confirmed years later and repeated publicly. But if it is not true then ... Oh! No wonder Hillary did not want investigators to have access to Foster's office because if Linda was "mistaken" would the Park Police/Fiske/- Starr/Clinger/Senate investigators have drawn a different conclusion?

Was Linda going to 'fess up, come clean, and admit to her "mistake" when she broke her silence? Well, sort of. Linda, naturally, had to protect herself. And here we were again. Linda wanted to tell the truth, she always *tried* to tell the truth, but she didn't have the guts or courage to do it. It would be like storytelling reminiscent of President Clinton's famous what-is-the-meaning-of-"is" silliness he used when he tried to dodge a perjury conviction in the Clinton-Lewinsky scandal and succeeded. Yes, I would include her "mistake," and other details I had accumulated when I wrote her story, and see if someone caught on and followed where her "mistake" went.

Finally, all the pieces were falling into place.

CW (the Confidential Witness) told us when he found Vince Foster's body at the Park, "Till this day I felt like I interrupted someone putting [Foster] there, and that there was someone there point blank when I was there because that gun did not fall out of a tree ... somebody put that gun in his hand."[238]

If Linda was "mistaken," did Vince Foster leave the White House with his briefcase and return to his office with his briefcase, where he committed suicide? Was Foster moved from the White House to Fort Marcy Park?

Wow! No wonder, at every stonewalled bend, every bizarre turn, while I researched the Foster case, I kept landing in the same spot, Foster's office, with the same question. What was in his office that Hillary and her lawyers did not want investigators to see? It could not have simply been privileged files (what remained of them) secured under lock and key, protected by attorney-client and executive privilege. Instead, did the Clinton White House refuse to allow investigators unfettered access to Foster's office because they could have found evidence that he had taken his life there—*blood, bone, brain matter, gun-shot residue,* had they been allowed to conduct a thorough search—one in which they collected forensic evidence?

Instantly, Linda's former supervisor, Pentagon spokesman Clifford Bernath's testimony during the Lewinsky investigation made sense. Bernath admitted during the Clinton-Lewinsky scandal that he had been contacted by a White House liaison requesting that a "good" job be created at the Pentagon for Linda. Bernath testified how Linda had told him that she "was involved in the Vince Foster affair." She knew "a lot of things" and she "made statements like, 'If you only knew' and I 'didn't want to know.'"[239]

*Wait! Slow down.*

I stopped and stalled my racing thoughts. *Don't jump to conclusions. It's a mistake/confession, not a smoking gun.*

To quote Bill Clinton: Was I trying to get blood out of a turnip? Would Hillary dismiss my findings as fiction and a desperate attempt to sell books and attack me personally? Yes. But the undeniable fact that remains is the Clintons have had years to fully cooperate with investigators and they did not—repeatedly, ever. The Clintons always, predictably, issue the same blanket denials, even when overwhelming evidence exists to the contrary—because they have to in order to stay in power. What is critically important and the only issue that matters is what does the evidence say.

Were the questionable, unethical and obstructive actions in the Clinton White House counsel's office after Foster died about keeping the Clintons' protected personal files out of investigators' hands—files they could not read? Or was Hillary's insistence (to her lawyers) on denying investigators access to Foster's office about preventing them from possibly finding remnants of Foster's blood or tissue in his office after he took his life there and was moved? Was a cleanup going on in Foster's office which would explain the wildly different Clinton White House death notification timeline discrepancies? Is that why nobody found the bullet in Fort Marcy Park, because the bullet was never there? Did Vince Foster commit suicide in his office?

Let's look at what the evidence tells us. Here is what we know:

At 5:59 p.m., when a 911 call reported that a dead body was discovered in Fort Marcy Park, we know senior staffers were working in the counsel's office. We know investigators were unable to pinpoint Foster's time of death. Nor could (or would) anyone account for his whereabouts after 1:00 p.m. until his body was found.

We know the Clinton White House stonewalled investigators, and staffers supplied conflicting testimony or suffered from bouts of "I can't recall" amnesia. We know the White House barred investigators from any meaningful access to Foster's office, an office that was already contaminated by Hillary's senior staff. And because Foster's office was not searched or tested for forensic evidence, *there is no evidence to rule out* the possibility that his office was *not* his place of death. We also know five government investigations drew conclusions using shoddy and incomplete evidence initially gathered at Fort Marcy Park by the Park Police.

*How could Foster be moved out of the White House and escape notice?*

If anyone knew how to leave the White House without detection, it was Hillary. "Occasionally, I snuck out of the White House wearing sweats, sunglasses and a baseball cap," Hillary wrote in her memoir, *Living History,* because she "loved looking through the Mall, looking at the monuments ..."[240]

One way to sneak out of the White House is by using the West Wing freight elevator. It is located a few paces from the counsel's office and stops at ground level. The elevator door opens outside where a car or delivery van can park to unload or load office supplies, furniture, anything. Because a person cannot access the freight elevator without first clearing through the White House security gates, there is no guard posted there. As soon as a delivery is completed, the driver can drive off and wave good-bye to the guards stationed at the gates without suspicion or concern.

We also know the freight elevator was not tested for forensics—therefore it cannot be ruled out that Foster's body was not in the elevator the day he was found dead.

If Foster took his life in his office shortly after the support staff had left for the day, he could have been transported out of the White House in the freight elevator and put into a trunk of a car or van that drove away without suspicion. Okay, moving on …

*If Foster shot himself in the White House does that explain why carpet fibers and hair belonging to somebody else were found on his body?*

We know from the official investigations that the most elementary component of evidence gathering was botched when Foster's clothing (bloodied and non-bloodied), was tossed into one evidence bag, "before trace evidence was collected," and "cannot be conclusively linked to particular items of clothing that Foster was wearing."[241]

Fiske provided us with another reason for the contamination: "Foster's clothes were laid out to dry for four days on the floor of a "photo lab room." This room is regularly used by Park Police officers working on investigations and is equipped with an exhaust fan. It is possible that the clothes were contaminated while in this room."[242]

So using the contaminated evidence, just like the investigators had to, we learn from Fiske's report: "Foster's clothing contained head hairs dissimilar from his own," and "carpet type fibers of various colors." Yet Fiske offered no explanation as to where the fibers came from or how they ended up on Foster.[243]

Starr elaborated in his report and found "two blond to light brown head hairs of Caucasian origin [that] were suitable for comparison purposes and dissimilar" to Foster.[244] But "the only known individuals ... to provide hair samples were persons already known to have had contact with Foster."[245]

According to the FBI report, "the FBI Laboratory found 35 definitive carpet-type fibers" from Foster's clothing. Of those fibers, 23 were white fibers ... 12 were various colors, which suggests 'those fibers did not originate from a single carpet.' The white fibers ... were consistent with carpet samples taken from Foster's home. The others, including blue-gray, blue, gold-brown, light-brown, gray, pink, and orange in color, were consistent with samples from the White House or his car. [246]

It was in March 1994, approximately *eight months* after Foster's death, when Fiske's investigators obtained "all available physical evidence collected in connection with the investigation of Foster's death, and provided it to the FBI Lab." The evidence included "the gun and the ammunition, Foster's clothing and eyeglasses, items found in Foster's car, photographs taken" at Fort Marcy Park and during "the autopsy, Foster's hair and blood samples, the autopsy report," and "portions of the Park Police Report."[247]

However, there is a critical deal that needs to be highlighted here: Hillary's extensive White House interior refurbishing and restorations project that began late in November 1992. Hillary with Kaki Hockersmith, a friend from Arkansas, spent nearly one year on the refurbishment that was financed by "private donations," totaling "$396,429.46."[248]

At the time, Linda said she did not think much about the White House refurbishing that was taking place (before, during, and after Foster's death) until I asked her about it. When I did, she paused, then crestfallen, recalled how the counsel's office renovation, including Foster's office, quickly proceeded after his death and included new paint and carpeting.

"They also took out Vince's furniture. Everything was ripped out and replaced." That means the samples the FBI took from the White House were not from the original carpeting in Foster's office.

In an announcement, the White House Office of the Press Secretary confirmed Linda's memory when they detailed the restorations and the renovations that occurred in the residence and in the West Wing. It included reupholstering, new paint, wood staining, new curtains, and carpets. Nineteen carpets and underlays "worn and needing attention," including the carpet on the second floor were replaced.[249] The counsel's office, Foster's office, is on the second floor.

Naturally, during the White House refurbishing and restoration project, carpets, carpet sections, and other equipment would be readily available that could have been used to protect Foster's head and his body—if he was moved. That would also explain how carpet fibers consistent with the White House and other carpets ended up on his body. A large rollaway garbage bin on wheels or other construction type dollies, also accessible during the refurbishing project, might have been used to transport his body out of the White House.

According to an independent Foster investigation conducted by Vincent J. Scalice, a veteran New York City Police homicide investigator, and an expert in crime scene reconstruction, identification, and forensic analysis, and Fred D. Santucci, a Forensic Photographer and Crime Scene Expert: "Carpet-type fibers of various colors which were found on almost all of Foster's clothing was clearly indicative of the fact that his body probably was in contact with one or more carpets. This evidence raises the possibility that his body may have been in a prone position, and/or his body may have been transported while in contact with some type of carpeting."[250]

### How could Foster get his gun into the White House?

Rather easily, actually. Starr's investigation reported that a kitchen oven mitt was found in the glove compartment of Foster's car. Foster's wife, Lisa, confirmed it was from their kitchen. She could not explain why it was in her husband's car.[251]

Dr. Lee examined the oven mitt and Foster's front-pant pockets and found the presence of sun flower husks and lead. "The presence of these trace materials could indicate they share a common origin," determined Dr. Lee. "This finding could indicate that an item which had gunshot residue on it, such as the revolver came in contact with the interior of [the oven mitt] and the "materials in the pants pocket clearly resulted from the transfer by an intermediate object, such as the Colt weapon."[252]

Investigators stated the weapon Foster used was a .38 Colt Army service revolver.

According to Starr's conclusion, the evidence surrounding Foster's gun was "consistent with a scenario in which Foster transported the gun from his home in the oven mitt and carried the gun in his pants pocket as he walked from his car in Fort Marcy Park."[253]

Operating under Starr's scenario, the evidence is also consistent that Foster could have transported the gun from his home in the oven mitt and carried the gun in his pant pocket as he walked from his car to his White House office where he killed himself.

As a senior staffer with a security pass (the coveted blue-pass with a "W" which meant unescorted access to the president and the West Wing), Foster (like Linda) was not required to go through the magnetometers every day when he went to work.

*If Foster committed suicide in the White House, how come nobody heard the shot?*

For the same reasons why nobody heard a gunshot at Fort Marcy Park.

Fiske's report tells us how neither individual interviewed the day Foster died heard a gunshot.[254] Starr suggested because the park is adjacent to the GW Parkway and Chain Bridge Road and "planes to and from National Airport regularly fly in patterns near the park" as another reason why nobody heard a gunshot. Fiske also noted that records obtained through the security guards at the Saudi residence, near Fort Marcy Park, "show that construction work ... was occurring at the residence on the date of Foster's death" as another possible reason why nobody heard the gun shot. [255]

In addition, Fiske determined: "the sound of the gun shot would've been further muffled by Foster shooting the gun inside his mouth."[256] We also know staffers apparently suffered from amnesia during the Foster inquiries and frequently testified that they couldn't recall much. Perhaps there were staffers who heard the gun shot.

*What about the White House press corps? Certainly, they would have seen or heard something.*

No. The press corps was in the basement, far away from the second floor counsel's office. Plus the corridor connecting the press room to the rest of the West Wing had been closed off shortly after the Clinton administration took office. "It was a plan cooked up by Hillary ..." Stephanopoulos explained in his excellent book, *All Too Human*. Hillary had said the president "wanted to be free to walk around without reporters looking over his shoulder."[257]

————

Let's walk back to Fort Marcy Park.

First, we know that no intensive review of the area under and around Foster's body "occurred on July 20, 1993, during the Park Police investigation."[258] We also know that no intensive or even mediocre review of Foster's White House office ever occurred.

According to the Fiske report, when the Park Police and Emergency Medical Services (EMS) personnel found Foster's body, "relatively little blood was visible."[259] That was highly unusual and suspect because the type of gun Foster used would have left a bloody, bloody, huge mess. Adding even more uncertainly to the belief that Foster shot himself at Fort Marcy Park, Fiske noted that "there was no blood spatter [sic] on the plants or trees surrounding the decedent's head."[260]

Because of the shoddy evidence gathering that occurred after Foster's body was found, investigators had no choice but to draw their conclusions with what they had, relying heavily on photographs that were taken at the scene. As previously noted, the 35-millimeter photographs were underexposed and of little value. The Polaroids, described as that of "greater investigative utility," consisted of thirteen Polaroids taken of the body scene and five taken of the parking lot—*that's it*.[261]

Starr reasoned that Foster died at Fort Marcy Park

because "substantially greater contamination of skin surfaces and clothing by spilled and/or smeared blood would have been unavoidable had the body been transported." [262] Sounds logical, except the Polaroids showed that *there was* contamination.

Fiske noted in his findings that the Polaroids showed "a larger area of blood staining Foster's right cheek and jaw, forming a "contact stain." [263]

Starr looked at the evidence and cited a "broad transfer-type blood smear was present at the right side of the chin and neck, precisely corresponding to a similar blood stain of the right collar area of the shirt."[264]

The FBI Lab Report concluded that Foster's head "moved or was moved after being in contact with the shoulder."[265]

But there was a big problem with that evidence because Foster's head was not in contact with his shoulder in the Polaroids that were taken at the scene. Furthermore, Foster was found lying "neatly" on his back, "facing virtually straight," and his arms were extended by his sides.[266] How then could the investigators explain the blood smears? They couldn't; so instead they were forced to make excuses once again.

"For obvious reasons," the investigators rationalized, Foster's "head *must have* [italics mine] been facing to the right when the body was found or have been turned to the right when the body was examined …"[267] Or could it be that the blood smear happened when Foster was moved?

The original theory the investigators depended upon ran into more problems, because there was more than one blood stain pattern on Foster's face; including a trail of blood that flowed upwards from his nose to above his ear.[268] This blood trail defied gravity because Foster's body was found on a steep embankment that sloped at about a 45-degree angle with his feet pointed down.[269] Therefore the investigators needed to rationalize some more. One theory suggested Foster's head was moved, more than once, by one of the "early observers." Another suggested that the stain occurred when an investigator checked to see if there was a pulse before the Polaroids were taken.[270]

Except the witnesses at Fort Marcy Park did not recall moving Foster's head, once, let alone more than once, including EMS worker Todd Stacey Hall. Hall said "he did not move Foster's head" when he checked for a pulse.[271] Therefore, applying the same logic as the investigators applied, could the contact stains have occurred when Foster's head hit his shoulder, more than once, when he was moved? This explanation would also explain how Foster's blood flowed upwards on his face when he was found dead lying on a downward slope.

Because of the absence of blood at the scene, believers of the official findings embraced evidence that "a pool of blood was found under [Foster's] head when the body was turned, and the upper back of his shirt was noted to be blood-soaked."[272] Fiske reported "when Foster's body was rolled over [Park Police investigators] observed a fairly large pool of blood on the ground."[273] Starr stated that Dr. Beyer, who prepared Foster's autopsy report, "found a large amount of blood in the body bag."[274]

However, we do not know how a fairly large pool or a large amount of blood was specifically quantified. The average male body holds between ten and twelve pints of blood.[275] That's between twenty and twenty-four cups of blood. Foster, at six feet and four-and-a-half inches tall, weighing 197 pounds, would qualify as above average. [276] How much blood is considered a "fairly large" or "large pool"?

There is more blood evidence that favors that

Foster might have been moved.

Forensic expert Dr. Henry Lee, after examining Foster's shoes, found that there were no heavy bloodstains or dripping type bloodstain patterns on them. Starr determined that Dr. Lee's finding would be contrary to "what might have been" had Foster's body been moved "in an upright position."[277]

Sounds logical, but would Dr. Lee's findings then not be contrary if Foster was moved horizontally? If he was, that would also explain the blood contact stains and smears. Could Foster have been transported by two people, or maybe three, who carried his body horizontally from underneath his shoulders and back area (while supporting his head) with another person carrying his legs?

Moreover, there are yet more problems with the official findings. How did Foster walk to the place where he was found dead considering, as Dr. Lee determined, "it was not possible to associate definitively any … soil material with Fort Marcy Park" in Foster's shoe soles?[278]

*Who moved Foster's body?*

It would not require a meticulously crafted nefarious plan to move Foster out of the White House, nor does one need to believe that a diabolical conspiracy plotted by a Clinton White House cabal existed either to thwart the outcome of the Foster findings. By moving one piece of evidence, particularly a key piece of evidence, is reminiscent to a game of dominos. Move one domino out of place, and all the dominos fall in a different direction. Moving one piece of evidence out of place would effectively alter the direction the investigators followed, and lead them to a different and inaccurate conclusion.

Like the investigators were forced to do, let's

explore the likely scenarios supported by the available evidence of who could have moved Foster out of the White House—if that's where he died.

There appear to be two possibilities.

First, because the discovery of Foster's body was officially reported to be near 6:00 p.m., we know senior staff in the counsel's office were working typical hours at the White House before and after his body was discovered. Second, consider the refurbishing work crews, who, like all temporary visitors, would be cleared into the White House through WAVES—Workers and Visitors Entry System—using social security number type screenings measures. Sound questionable? For starters, speak to the over "one hundred and twenty-two congressional witnesses who invoked their Fifth Amendment right against self-incrimination, or to the people who fled the country to avoid testifying" in other Clinton investigations to see precisely how viable this scenario really is.[279] Remember they would have been up against the most powerful couple in the world.

Imagine you were in the counsel's office, late afternoon on July 20. You heard a gunshot and panic-raced into Foster's office to find him dying. What would you do? Most people would call the police, an ambulance, or both. But as previously demonstrated in *The Whistleblower*, the Clinton White House avoided investigators and the authorities like vampires fleeing the light. And when investigators were unavoidable, they were stonewalled, obstructed, denied access and the ability to perform their jobs effectively, plus their subpoenas were ignored.

With little time to react and no time to plan, one should seriously consider the person(s), who thought fast on their feet, who held great power and influence. Who could have triggered such a hurried chain reaction to move Foster out of the White House?

According to the Senate Whitewater committee investigation on June 30, 1995, almost two years after Foster's death, the committee "requested from the White House records reflecting communications that took place between 5:00 p.m. on July 20 and 5:00 p.m. on July 22, 1993 from or to Hillary"— including telephone records.

As usual the Clinton White House did not respond until a second request for the documentation was repeated, and then "approximately three months after" the initial request "the Clinton's personal attorney produced records of Mrs. Clinton's telephone calls from the Rodham residence."[280]

But Hillary was not at the Rodham residence when Foster's body was found near 6:00 p.m. Hillary was flying from the West coast to D.C. when she, by her own account, "between 8:00-9:00 p.m." stopped in Arkansas "to drop off her mother and visit some friends."[281]

That meant investigators were given telephone records that did not cover the critical time frame— before Foster's body was discovered. Had the White House readily produced Hillary's phone records from 5:00 p.m. onward, including the calls made from or to Hillary when she was airborne, we would know whether or not Hillary could be ruled out, but they did not. Therefore Hillary cannot be ruled out.

Could Foster have been moved out of the White House by less than a handful of people, who were at the wrong place, at the wrong time, who would not dare say, "no"? Individuals, who might have followed orders that came from a very high and an intimidating place? Could one phone call have possibly started it all? Remember, if this scenario is accurate, for the persons involved in the Foster cover-up, to say "no" they would be challenging the leader of the free world, and his wife, the co-president.

———

*Did Foster drive his car to Fort Marcy Park?*

When two Park Police agents watched investigator Rolla search Foster's body for personal effects at Fort Marcy Park the investigators watched Rolla remove a "watch, pager, and two rings."[282] As part of his search, Rolla "felt into" Foster's pant pockets, which were empty. Foster's car keys were nowhere to be found.

Well, then how did Foster drive his car to Fort Marcy Park if he did not have his car keys? He could not, so the investigators had to rationalize once again.

Starr's report ultimately accepted a revised explanation that Rolla "did not reach to the bottom of [Foster's] suit pants pockets."[283]

Seemed like a harmless oversight, right?

Except when the Park Police investigators realized they did not have Foster's car keys, they went to the morgue to research the body. Not only did the investigators locate Foster's car keys in his right pant pocket but they also found a second set of keys with four door and cabinet keys.[284] Foster's right pant pocket was near "his right waist area," where Rolla retrieved his pager during the initial search.[285] How could he have missed them?

Was it wishful thinking that two sets of keys could have been so easily overlooked during a suicide/homicide investigation?

We have two choices here. Either we believe that Rolla was astonishingly sloppy and inept during his initial search of Foster's body, or he was telling the truth and Foster did not have his car keys. If the latter is true then it was impossible for Foster to have driven to Fort Marcy Park. [286]

The seething conspiracy beast was provoked again when conflicting accounts surfaced as to who arrived at the morgue first—was it White House staffers or the investigators? Using the evidence from the initial body search, and not bending it like a pretzel, lends credence that someone else, other than Foster, drove his car to Fort Marcy Park, and it also explains why Foster's car keys were not found in his pockets during the initial search at the park.

*How did carpet fibers "consistent" with a car end up on Foster's body?*

Details matter. It is hard to imagine anyone, let alone a man like Foster, at six feet, four-and-a-half inches in height, lying down in a car trunk, but we must imagine he did because somehow carpet fibers "consistent" with a car ended up on his body. Starr's report stated there was "no evidence that a body had been" in Foster's car trunk," so the question remains how did car carpet fibers end up on Foster?[287]

If Foster was moved, then we know how it happened, and possibly there was more than one person who handled the task of moving him. Consider that someone else may have driven Foster's car, and another person drove *their own car* with Foster in their trunk (a car that has never been located or forensically tested).

If Foster was moved, one might assume that the movers would not want to walk home after placing Foster neatly on an embankment in Fort Marcy Park. If Foster was transported in somebody else's car that would explain how carpet fibers "consistent" with a car, the White House, and other carpets, were found on his body.[288]

*How could Foster have been transported from the parking lot to the cannon in the Fort Marcy Park and escape notice?*

As journalist Michael Iskioff observed in *Slate*, "To have transported the deputy White House counsel's lumpy dead body 200 yards from the parking lot to the cannon and have nobody notice would have been quite an achievement."

I agree, but the evidence shows it was possible.

Here's how: Starr's report noted that the "trees, brush and hills within the park were such that one would not walk in an absolutely straight line from the parking lot to the second cannon." The second cannon was located out of sight from the clear grassed-ground and secluded high atop a berm enclosed by trees and brush. Also, "trees and thick vines" were "growing through a fence" that "outlines the northern side of Fort Marcy Park" and "blocks vehicles from entering but not pedestrians."[289]

Anyone who has visited Fort Marcy Park, as I have, knows if a person walked from the cemented parking lot to the wide dirt path (wide enough for vehicles), up the inclines to the second cannon, there is a densely wooded area with an abundance of trees outlining the multileveled hilled park. Brush and other dense summer foliage provide additional privacy, creating more than one possible route to have taken.

Foster's body could have been moved in the area beneath the sharp angle of the berms, for instance, concealed by the densely wooded area. As noted previously: "No record of any effort to canvass the neighborhood near the time of death to determine whether anyone had seen or heard relevant information" occurred. Maybe someone did see something.[290]

*Where is the fatal bullet?*

Unknown. As noted earlier, the Park Police investigators and Fiske's and Starr's investigators all searched Fort Marcy Park and could not find the bullet that killed Foster.[291]

If Foster died in Fort Marcy Park by shooting himself at close range, one must ask how far the bullet could have gone. According to the autopsy, "the point of entry" of the bullet "was in the back of [Foster's] mouth with the exit in the back of [Foster's] head."[292]

The investigators could not explain what happened to the bullet either, so once again excuses were required. They ultimately decided that there was a "distinct possibility" that the bullet ricocheted "off a natural or man -made obstruction."[293] Because investigators were denied access to Foster's White House office, one cannot prove or disprove whether or not a bullet was fired there or was there.

# 12

# The Death of

# Vince Foster

"For as by one man's disobedience many were
made sinners, so by the obedience of one shall
many be made righteous."

**—Romans 5:19 (KJV)**

So what happened to Vince Foster? Consider this
scenario.

At 4:30 p.m., on July 20, 1993, according to an
eyewitness, Foster's car was not at the parking lot at
Fort Marcy Park.[294]

It was around 5:00 p.m. when the support staff left
for the day and headed for home. Shortly thereafter
Foster may have returned to the White House counsel's
suite after having eaten a big meal earlier that might
have been "meat and potatoes" (which could also
account for his missing whereabouts that afternoon).[295]

Conceivably, he acknowledged his colleague(s),
who naturally were hard at work and very relieved to see
him. Perhaps Foster went inside his office where he
dropped his briefcase by his desk, adjusted his
eyeglasses before he reached inside his right pant pocket
to retrieve the gun. His deceiving thoughts riddled with
agonizing blackness could not see mercy, salvation,
light, or Jesus, when he placed the .38 caliber revolver
muzzle inside his mouth, and pulled the trigger.[296]

The bang of the gunshot propelled Lawyer #1 on a race he could not win. Entering the threshold of Foster's office, Lawyer #1 could not believe his eyes; his colleague, his admired friend had shot himself. He was bleeding, dying.

Shocked, Lawyer #1 grabbed the phone to call for help, 911, when his Clinton lawyer-ingrained reflexes took over (remember law enforcement is the enemy, on perpetual fishing expeditions to destroy the Clintons). His finger dialed another number instead and he was connected to X. *Who would know what to do? Who would have been livid had they not been notified first and protected?*

With a devastated, upset voice Lawyer #1 relayed the harrowing news about Foster's suicide to a stunned voice, X, on the other end of the line. X's voice might have become very, very angry and shrill. X, who notably thought fast on their feet, unleashed a sharp round of orders to get Foster out of the White House—now! The Clintons could not risk having a crime scene investigation in his office. Not with Foster charged to protect 'the client' instead of the American people. That "can of worms" must not be opened—ever.[297]

Lawyer #1 might have tried to argue but there was no time to reason with a belligerent, intimidating X. He felt cornered, trapped. *The ends justify the means ...* Lawyer #1's face was not conspiratorial but instead it betrayed the survivor instinct within him because as X made abundantly clear: the fate and future of the Clinton administration was at stake, and if he didn't follow orders there would be hell to pay. Perhaps Lawyer #1 knew, just like Foster knew, how X had to be protected at "all costs."[298] *"Hurry! Get him the f—k out! The freight elevator! Grab his keys, the gun. Get his car!*

Lawyer #1 may have struggled to recover his composure. It is possible that his soul might have been battered and weary after months of the constant, never-ending onslaught of Clinton damage control that had become his life, but he did not dare defy the orders. Nobody, absolutely nobody ever does. Was he convincing himself that what had been asked of him was in the best interests of the country, his best interests, or someone else's? *Hurry!*

The selection of who may have moved Foster out of the White House was swift. They were not picked because of their physical strength or because they were cursed with wicked minds; they were chosen because they were now bound by an unspeakable, secret allegiance. They were possibly the White House staffers who worked typically long hours who heard the shot and rushed inside Foster's office to find him at death's door.

Inside the counsel's office a frenzy of activity followed. How many people would have been needed— two, three, five? Lawyer #1 repeated his ordered checklist to the small group. What could have been the words he had used? *Critical mission, classified, in the interest of your country ... you have been asked on behalf of the president of the United States...* Perhaps a trusted White House aide (Man#1) had been notified by X to assist, and he was already en route with his car to wait outside the freight elevator exit to help move Foster out of the White House.

Did it take two, perhaps three (Man #2, Man #3) or more people to lower Foster horizontally onto a carpet (which is when carpet that "was consistent" with the White House ended up on his clothing), and then place him in a rollaway garbage bin or construction dolly? The accessible carpets used during Hillary's White House refurbishing project would have prevented Foster's blood from trickling onto the floor and later in Fort Marcy Park. *Distract the patrolling foot soldiers. Check that the coast was clear.*

If true, Foster would have been transported quickly from his office to the freight elevator. Although, it must have felt like forever, it only took a couple of minutes for the elevator door to open outside to Man #1, who was waiting in a car that was possibly blue.[299]

When Foster's body was lowered into the trunk, was that when carpet fibers consistent with a car rubbed onto his clothes?[300]

Perhaps, afterwards, Man #3 took off to the White House parking lot to get Foster's car, as Man #2 jumped into Man #1's car. *"Meet you at the park ... "*

Perhaps because Foster was tall, they lowered and placed him on an angle and that was when his head collided with his shoulder, causing the shirt stain that covered the top of his "shoulder from the neck to the top of the arm" and consisted "of saturating stains typical of having been *caused by a flow of blood onto or soaking into the fabric* [italics mine]."[301]

Foster's blood could have continued to soak through his dress shirt as the car he was transported in, driven by Man #1 with Man #2, drove through the White House gates, with no suspicion, towards Fort Marcy Park.

Meanwhile inside Foster's office it would have been a bloody mess (unlike how it would be at Fort Marcy Park) and the cleanup was underway. How many people would it take to scrub it down? One? Two? Three? The lawyer(s) possibly left them in Foster's office to finish the cleanup job and raced directly to different public restaurants for dinner because when the calls came in to notify the White House of Foster's shocking death, alibis would be absolutely necessary.

Now we may know why White House lawyers cut short their characteristically "long, intense, and demanding hours of work," on a day when an admired and adored colleague and friend went missing.[302]

Meanwhile, the car with Foster in its trunk was headed to Fort Marcy Park. Man #1 and #2 (or more) could have been frustrated by the traffic. Fort Marcy Park is less than an eight-mile drive from the White House. An easy fifteen-minute drive but allowing for traffic, the car could have been at Fort Marcy Park in less than thirty minutes.[303]

At Fort Marcy Park, at 5:15 p.m., two witnesses, a couple, pulled in. They sat in their car in the parking lot for "approximately 15 minutes before going into the woods." They did not see Foster's car in the parking lot.[304]

After 5:30 p.m., the car transporting Foster arrived at the park. The driver had more than one route to choose from to pick a location to leave the body. Perhaps the car turned onto the dirt back road and headed behind the hills when they spotted the berm and cannon and parked. As Man #1 and Man #2 lifted Foster out of the trunk, possibly Foster's head dropped backwards, which would explain the blood on his face that flowed upwards, defying gravity.[305] But the carpet had been especially helpful when Man #1 and Man #2 carried Foster, hammock-styled, up the embankment, taking hurried steps up the hill toward the cannon.

Deciding on a spot, the men eased Foster's body off the tarp, placing him neatly down, and virtually straight onto the steep slope. One man placed a wine cooler nearby. But in their urgent haste, Man #1 and Man #2 might have left the gun and Foster's eyeglasses in the car (obviously they did not have his car keys). They had to go back to the car and get them. It was around 5:45 p.m. when perhaps Man #1 was returning to finish what they had started when he froze because someone else was there, looking at Foster's body. It was CW, the confidential witness.

Perhaps it was then that a startled Man #1 dropped
Foster's eyeglasses onto the ground 13 feet below his
feet and then hid.[306] Man #1 would have had to wait for
the stranger to leave to complete the task of putting the
gun in Foster's hand. Perhaps he hid behind the dense
foliage or behind the huge tree that grew below the
second cannon.

In order to believe the official findings, one must
accept that if Foster fired the gun in Fort Marcy Park,
the fierce impact threw his eyeglasses off of his face,
and his glasses "bumped" down the berm 19 feet from
his head, while his body miraculously fell neatly down
and virtually straight onto the slope with a gun
remaining in his hand. [307]

Above the embankment, CW was staring at
Foster's body. *Was he sleeping? No. There's blood.* His eyes
focused downward looking for a weapon but there was
"no gun, no sign of a weapon. It looked like [Foster]
had been placed there." The key to it was when CW
"saw the leaves trampled down below [Foster's waist
area]" and lots of "foot traffic at the bottom of the hill."
[308]

But that day at Fort Marcy Park, CW had sensed
that he was not alone either. He had felt like he
"interrupted someone putting him there. And there was
someone there point blank when" he was there. Indeed,
Man #1, holding Foster's gun, could have been waiting
nearby among the dense foliage.

Was it after CW fled to his van to report the dead
body that Man #1 may have hurried to the body and
placed the gun in Foster's right hand? It would have
been too risky for Man #1 to have done anything else
because someone had seen Foster's body. *They might be
reporting it now* …. Man #1 raced back to the car to meet
up with Man #2. Later CW told investigators:
"Someone put that gun in [Foster's] hand."[309]

Meanwhile, before 6:00 p.m. Man #3, driving Foster's car, perhaps had already pulled into Fort Marcy Park and parked. Man #3 waited impatiently for Man #1 and Man #2 to come pick him up and to give them Foster's car keys.

Luckily, Man #3 did not have to wait long because the first person known to have seen a light gray car parked where Foster's light gray Honda was found, reported seeing it at about six o'clock. The witness also saw a blue car (the blue car was never located or forensically tested).[310]

Man #1 perhaps told Man #3: *Someone spotted the body already. It's too risky for us to go back with his car keys. F—k-it, we'll deal with it later.* And they drove away shortly before the authorities arrived. Several witnesses at Fort Marcy Park were never located, including the person(s) in the blue car.[311]

When Park Police investigators arrived that hot summer day, hovering around 92 degrees, at 6:35 p.m., some of Foster's blood on his face was "wet" and "starting to dry" and "there were no signs of rigor mortis," suggesting that Foster died not long before he was found.[312] Investigators never explained why they couldn't pinpoint his time or approximate time of death.

If Foster killed himself in his office, was it possible that he was moved from the White House to Fort Marcy Park in less than an hour?

Meanwhile, back at the White House inside Foster's office, it could have been a bloody mess, and could have taken a couple hours to clean up. It was "shortly after 7:00 p.m.," when those tasked with the cleanup possibly "switched off the intruder alarm in the counsel's office" and left. [313] The intruder alarm could have been switched on earlier during the cleanup to alert the cleanup people if someone was coming.

Perhaps, during the cleanup, the cleanup people destroyed evidence, grabbed the bullet (that was never located by investigators) and the suicide note—a real one that Foster actually wrote himself, before they notified a White House point man that their critical mission on behalf of their country and the most powerful people in the world was complete.

At shortly before 9:00 p.m., "a young female makeup artist working for *CNN*," was preparing President Clinton in the White House Map room for an appearance on *Larry King* when "an unidentified male, whom she presumed to be an aide" came in and "notified Clinton that a note or document had been found in Foster's office."[314]

The *CNN* make-up artist told Fiske's investigators about the exchange. For reasons unknown, the exchange was omitted from the official reports as was the note or document that was found in Foster's office after he killed himself.

Now we may know why the Clinton White House quickly announced that Foster committed suicide in Fort Marcy Park before a preliminary investigation began—*because they knew all along what had really happened to him.*

Now we may know why President Clinton repeatedly said Foster's death would remain a mystery and why, "We'll just have to live with something else we can't understand"—*because the Clintons made sure we would never find out.*

Now we may know why the Clintons attacked, maligned, denounced, and thwarted the investigators and journalists who dared to try to find out the truth about Foster's death—including the motivations behind his decision—and seek justice.[315]

*What was so bad? What were you afraid of—afraid we would find out?*

Now we may know why "law enforcement officials were confronted at every turn with concerted efforts to deny them access to evidence in Mr. Foster's office," and why despite having made an agreement with the attorney general of the United States regarding gaining access to Foster's office, the agreement was broken and instead "the counsel to the president carried out the wishes of the First Lady."[316] Why? *To conceal what had tormented Foster, tasked with keeping the Clintons handcuff free, including Whitewater—"a can of worms you shouldn't open."*[317]

Now we may also know why Hillary and Bill Clinton never once expressed any outrage, sorrow, disgust, or dismay at what was the undeniable and non-debatable shoddy evidence gathering (or lack thereof) that occurred during the investigation at Fort Marcy Park and where Foster was last seen alive at the White House—something any decent person of minimal conscience would have done for their "best" friend and trusted colleague *if they didn't know* what really happened to them.

According to Starr's report, "based on all of the available evidence: Vince Foster committed suicide by gun-shot in Fort Marcy Park on July 20, 1993."[318]

With the addition of Linda's corrected "mistake;" it is possible that based on the available evidence: Vince Foster committed suicide by gunshot in his White House office, and was moved to Fort Marcy Park on July 20, 1993.

Again, unlike the five official investigations, this finding explains what was in Foster's office that Hillary and the Clinton lawyers did not want investigators to see, and why investigators were stonewalled, obstructed, and denied access to his office at every turn.

Linda once said to me, "I know this is going to sound strange, but sometimes I think Hillary knows more than I do [about Foster's death], and I was in the counsel's office."

Never once did I receive a clear indication as to whether or not Linda knew if Foster shot himself in his office but her Foster briefcase "mistake," her repeated justifications, and defensive dodges, and the fact that *she was a Clinton team-player*, instead suggest a troubling conclusion. By following the Clinton White House orders to keep her job, Linda, the reviled (or revered) so-called whistleblower of impeachment fame, contributed to what unquestionably was the Foster cover-up.

As she had testified during the Clinton-Lewinsky investigation: "I had reason to believe that the Vince Foster tragedy was not depicted accurately under oath by members of the administration ... and these are, remember, instances of national significance that included testimony by, also, Mrs. Clinton, also in Travelgate. It became very important for them for their version of events to be the accepted version of events. I knew based on my personal knowledge, personal observations that they were lying under oath. So it became very fearful for me that I had information even back then that was very dangerous." [319]

Linda's reason to believe the official narrative was false, in part, could be because she wasn't truthful either—by mistake of course. Wink ... *Following Orders* ...

Everything you were told to believe about the Clinton investigations is upside down.

Finally, I understood the silencing ammunition the Clintons had over her, where, aside from salacious scandal and inferences, Linda's federal-immunity-protected lips remained selectively stapled-shut during the Clinton-Lewinsky impeachment investigation. Now, I understood why she had silently suffered through the vicious politics of personal destruction that captivated the nation for almost a year in 1998, for reasons she could never explain.

Instantly her reasons for wanting insurance to protect herself from the Clintons years later when she tape-recorded her conversations with President Bill Clinton's paramour, Monica Lewinsky, to avoid lying in *another court* case the Clintons *were attempting to fix* were crystal clear. Linda Tripp did not want to cover-up for the Clinton regime ever again, and lose her job, again— she had already done so before by following orders.

Let us remember it was in 1994, as reported in *The Whistleblower*, despite having been a Clinton team-player, following their orders, and testifying as she had been coached to do, she was still kicked out of the White House "wearing a smile" after she began asking questions. Stripped of the careerist protections she had previously enjoyed, which would have permitted her to serve under future administrations, the Clinton White House had pacified her with a Pentagon promotion and a hefty salary increase to about $100,000 a year. She took it. They owned her. She knew it.

"I had no choice. The Clinton White House knew it and so did I. I needed the job and you better believe I played by their rules. Everybody else did," Linda had said to me.[320]

*Everybody else did.*

If Bill and Hillary Clinton went down, she would go down too and to avoid that fate she had admittedly lived her life as a slave to sin instead of seeking redemption and justice.

Time and time again fear and intimidation spoke when Linda served in the Clinton administration. She had listened and obeyed their orders to save her job. The irony is at the very end, she lost it. She allowed her fear of man—not of God—to betray her conscience and to betray justice for Vince and for the American people. Had the Clinton administration been held accountable back then, imagine how history might have been spared all the Clinton scandals that were yet to come: from Whitewater to Chinagate to impeachment to Pardongate; then to the deadly Fast and Furious, Wikileaks, and Benghazi-Gate in the Obama White House in which Hillary serves as Secretary of State.

Washington is broken. Both sides of the political aisle— Republican and Democrats are compromised or feckless. Do not be deceived. Unfortunately, Linda wasn't unique in Washington or in civil service and elsewhere. She was not the only person who succumbed to the Clintons' (or other people of power's) best interests at her expense or at the expense of the truth and justice, nor would she be the last. Now is the time to take a stand, either chose to speak the truth, and seek redemption, or remain corrupt and lawless.

*Conscience.* As Vince Foster so eloquently, prophetically, and correctly stated before his death about what happened to people serving in the Clinton administration: "Before we came here, we thought of ourselves as good people." RIP.

We end now as we began, "Take no part in the unfruitful works of darkness, but instead expose them." —Ephesians 5:11 ESV

# Epilogue

"What will you do in the day of punishment,
And in the desolation which will come from afar?
To whom will you flee for help?
And where will you leave your glory?"

**—Isaiah 10:3 (NKJV)**

Two months after Foster's death Jerry Luther Parks, who worked closely with Foster, was shot dead while driving home from a restaurant in Arkansas. Parks had worked for the Clintons for years and was put in charge of security at the 1992 Clinton-Gore campaign headquarters in Little Rock. As his wife confirmed, her husband "had carried out sensitive assignments for the Clinton circle for almost a decade, and the person who gave him his instructions was Vince Foster." (The Parks home had also been burglarized a week after Foster's death and all of Parks' files on the Clintons were stolen).[321] As of this writing, his murder remains unsolved and the killer at large.

Foster's assistant Deb Gorham, and Betsy Pond left the White House shortly after Foster's death. Bernie Nussbaum paid for the honor and privilege of serving in the Clinton White House by resigning in disgrace, humiliated. Webster Hubbell's price for serving and protecting the Clintons forever branded him a convicted felon who spent 18 months in prison. Linda went on to become the most hated person in America (and the world) during the Lewinsky-Clinton scandal according to the press.[322] She was also charged with wire-tapping in the State of Maryland for recording her conversations with Monica Lewinsky (the criminal charges were eventually dropped).[323] Her FBI files were illegally leaked to the press (the case was ultimately settled in her favor). Naturally, in the upside-down world that became America under the Clintons' progressive 'the ends justify the means' regime, the taxpayers, not the Clintons, paid the $595,000 settlement.[324]

Meanwhile, Hillary won the Senate seat in New York although she, as I reported in *The Whistleblower,* was continually found to be "factually" inaccurate with investigators during all the Clinton investigations (otherwise known as perjury for you or me). When she ran for president in 2007, she happily, repeatedly declared that she had foreign policy credentials and was ready to be commander-and-chief on day-one because she had dodged sniper fire when she was in Bosnia. It would take another tape, this time a video tape to expose yet another Clinton lie.[325] Her reward for thwarting the rule of law and lying to America and the world was the honor of serving as President Obama's Secretary of State.

With Hillary as President Obama's secretary of state, America's prestige and strength plummeted. The biggest breach to America's national security occurred under Hillary's watch when WikiLeaks leaked hundreds of thousands of State Department cables on the Internet, damaging U.S. diplomacy efforts worldwide and endangering countless lives. As of this writing no senior official has been held to account.[326]

During the gun-running operation investigation "Fast and Furious," where countless Mexicans and U.S. Border Patrol Agent Brian Terry have been murdered by weapons the Justice Department allowed into Mexico, Hillary's State Department stonewalled investigators.[327]

In 2009, when the people of Iran rose up against the oppressive and vehemently anti-American Iranian regime (the largest state sponsor of terrorism), the Obama-Clinton so-called smart-power foreign policy opted not to "meddle," and watched the Iranian people literally be slaughtered.[328]

When corrupt people successfully thwart the rule of law and are never held to account, they are emboldened to continue to break the law. Without consulting the American people and without Congressional support, the Obama-Clinton regime sent U.S. troops into Libya to overthrow Dictator Col. Moammar Gadhafi.[329] Their so-called smart-power foreign policy emboldened America's sworn enemies and overthrew allies in the Middle East from Egypt to Tunisia.[330] Thanks to their "Arab Spring" the Muslim Brotherhood are growing in power. Currently, Christians in the Middle East are fleeing their homeland to avoid certain persecution or death.[331] Meanwhile Hillary and Obama, who both profess to be Christians, remain silent on their deadly plight.

*By their fruits you shall know them.*

On September 11, 2012, a terrorist attack in Benghazi, Libya, killed four Americans: Ambassador Christopher Stevens, former Navy SEALs Glen Doherty, Tyrone Woods and Sean Smith, a computer expert. Hillary was among the first top Obama administration officials to mislead the public by erroneously blaming a YouTube video as the cause of the attack.[332] Even more disturbing, we now know the Obama-Clinton regime watched the terrorist attack take place via live feeds and declined life-saving requests for help. The deadly cover-up continues.[333]

As of this writing, Hillary reportedly plans to step down as Secretary of State shortly after President Obama's second inauguration. This move would not only provide her with legal cover during the Benghazi investigations where she can lawyer-up as a civilian, (thus far Hillary, as a government employee, has declined to testify before Congress citing "scheduling conflicts" that includes wine tastings in Australia), and give her time to prepare and re-craft herself as a "moderate" for an anticipated 2016 Presidential run. After all, as reported in *The Whistleblower*, it is part of the "master plan."[334]

President Bill Clinton would later become the "President of the World" according to *MSNBC*, and launch the Clinton Global Initiative (CGI) to "solve the world's most pressing problems."[335] The truth is some of the people who were responsible for creating the world's problems attend the CGI. Individuals from Citigroup and AIG, for example, both played leading roles in the economic crisis and then took government bailouts—both have also sponsored CGI.[336] Coincidence? It was President Clinton with the help of a Republican Congress who repealed Glass-Steagall, which had previously prevented banks from becoming casinos and had safeguarded America in part from an economic crash.[337]

As the chief campaigner and fundraiser for President Obama's 2012 reelection campaign, Clinton was the key-note speaker at the Democrat National Convention and put Obama's name into nomination.[338] There is no doubt that Clinton's support played a pivotal role in President Obama's 2012 re-election. As of this writing, he, along with former Democratic New Jersey Governor and Goldman Sachs chief Jon Corzine (and former Obama fundraiser) have currently dodged justice or any accountability in the MF Global brokerage firm collapse where about "$1 billion in customer money" vanished.[339]

So truth fails, and he who departs from evil makes himself a prey. Then the Lord saw it, and it displeased

Him that there was no justice. (Isaiah 59:15 NKJV)
America … please … wake up.

MARINKA PESCHMANN

## A note to my secular, atheist, agnostic, and humanist friends and readers

We are all free to believe or to *not believe* in God. With or without the Bible verses, *Following Orders* is the same story. If you have a problem with references to God and to Christianity skip over the scriptures that open each chapter. When reporting on politicians who adhere to an ideology dedicated to Lucifer, I believe it is prudent to counter Lucifer with God. That said, I think it is fair to say we are all flawed. I also believe that a liar and a hypocrite, be it a person "of faith" or a "non-believer," is still a liar and a hypocrite just like corruption, whether it appears on the right or the left of the political spectrum, is still corruption.

## A note on sourcing and documentation

The quotes in this book are real unless otherwise cited as a reconstruction. They come from my personal notes, research, and tapes. Occasionally they are from secondary printed media sources that are sourced in the endnotes. Please visit: marinkapeschmann.com for additional sourcing, videos, documentation, resources, and contact information.

## A comprehensive, though not exhaustive, bibliography

Several books have been written about the Clinton era and the Foster case. They have all proved invaluable, most notably: Bill and Hillary Clinton's autobiographies, *My Life* and *Living History; All Too Human—a political education*, by George Stephanopoulos; *Sell Out*, by David Schippers; *My FBI*, by Louis J. Freeh; *For Love of Politics:*

142

*Bill and Hillary Clinton: The White House Years*, by Sally Bedell Smith; *Monica's Story*, by Andrew Morton; *The Strange Death of Vincent Foster*, by Christopher Ruddy; The Office of Independent Counsel's investigations; Senate Whitewater Committee investigations; and White House press briefings.

## Additional Resources and Official Reports

- Investigation of Whitewater Development and Related Matters Final Report, June 17, 1996, access online at: www.washingtonpost.com/wp-srv/politics/special/whitewater/committee.pdf
- Whitewater: Foster Report (note: This is the full text of the report on the 1993 death of White House counsel Vincent W. Foster, Jr., compiled by Whitewater independent counsel Kenneth Starr via *Washington Post*, access online at: www.washingtonpost.com/wp-srv/politics/special/whitewater/docs/foster.htm.
This file does not contain the report's footnotes or appendix.)
- Starr Report. Independent counsel Kenneth Starr's report to the House on President Clinton. Editor's Note: Some of the language in these documents is sexually explicit. www.washingtonpost.com/wp-srv/politics/special/clinton/icreport/icreport.htm

# ABOUT THE AUTHOR

**MARINKA PESCHMANN**, the author of *The Whistleblower: How the Clinton White House Stayed in Power to Reemerge in the Obama White House and on the World Stage (One Rock Ink)*, is a freelance journalist. She has collaborated, ghostwritten, and contributed to books and stories from showbiz and celebrities to true crime, politics, and the United Nations. After freelancing behind the scenes in both the mainstream press and the new media, it was time to step forward.

# ENDNOTES

### Prologue

[1] Kenneth W. Starr, Independent Counsel, *Report on the Death of Vincent W. Foster*, October 10, 1997, p.64.

[2] Robert B. Fiske Jr., Special Prosecutor, *Fiske Report*, June 30, 1994, see CW (Confidential Witness).

[3] Jason DeParle, "A Life Undone—A special report; Portrait of a White House Aide Ensnared by His Perfectionism," *New York Times,* August 22, 1993; access online at:
http://www.nytimes.com/1993/08/22/us/life-undone-special-report-portrait-white-house-aide-ensnared-his-perfectionism.html?pagewanted=1

[4] Clinton White House *Press Briefing*, July 22, 1993; access online at: http://clinton6.nara.gov/1993/07/1993-07-22-press-briefing-by-dee-dee-myers.html

[5] *Merriam-Webster Dictionary*, (Encyclopedia Britannica Company, 2012).

[6] *Final Report of Senate Whitewater Investigation*, June 13, 1996, p. 22; access online at: http://www.washingtonpost.com/wp-srv/politics/special/whitewater/committee.pdf

[7] Hillary Clinton, *Living History*, (First Schibner, Trade paperback edition, 2004) p. 297.

[8] "Fast and Furious" a "Catastrophic Disaster:" Border agents criticize weapons program," 'Chairman Darrell Issa, the House Oversight and Government Reform Committee, *CSPAN,* June 15, 2011. Also see: Stephen Dinan and Chuck Neubauer, "Issa: Obama admin intimidating witnesses in ATF gun probe,"

*Washington Times*, July 26, 2011. Also see: Sharyl Attkisson,

"Emails detail unfolding Benghazi attack on September 11,"
*CBS News*, October 23, 2012; access online:
http://www.cbsnews.com/8301-18563_162-57538689/emails-detail-unfolding-benghazi-attack-on-sept-11/

9 John F. Kennedy, *The President and the Press: American Newspaper Publishers Association*, Waldorf-Astoria Hotel, New York, April 27, 1961, transcript available online at:
http://www.cuttingthroughthematrix.com/transcripts/JFK_Video_Speech.html

10 Jane Mayer, "Portrait of a Whistleblower," *New Yorker Magazine*, March 23, 1998. Also see: "The Privacy Act of 1974," *Justice Department*, updated September 26, 2003; access online at:
http://www.justice.gov/opcl/privstat.htm. Also see: "Defense Department Settles with Linda Tripp," *Associated Press*, November 3, 2003; access online at:
http://www.usatoday.com/news/washington/2003-11-03-tripp-lawsuit_x.htm. Also see: Helen Kennedy, "Md Prosecutors Drop Tripp Wiretapping Charges," *New York Daily News*, May 25, 2000.

11 Peter Slevin, "For Clinton and Obama, a Common Ideological Touchstone," *Washington Post*, March 25, 2007; access online at:
http://www.washingtonpost.com/wp-dyn/content/article/2007/03/24/AR2007032401152.html

12 Saul Alinsky, *Rules for Radicals*, (Vintage, October 23, 1989).

**Chapter 1: It Does Not Take a Village**

13 "The President under Fire;" excerpts from interview with Hillary Clinton on *NBC's Today Show*, January 28, 1998; access online at: http://www.nytimes.com/1998/01/28/us/the-president-under-fire-excerpts-from-interview-with-mrs-clinton-on-nbc.html

14 "Clinton Accused. Key Player: Paula Jones," *Washington Post*, October 2, 1998; access online at:
http://www.washingtonpost.com/wp-srv/politics/special/clinton/players/jones.htm

[15] Linda Tripp, *Starr Report, Part III*, p. 4276, see July 28, 1998, p. 46. "I felt that it was an insurance policy so that it would be more difficult for them to fire me because they didn't like what I was saying under oath."

[16] Linda Tripp, *Starr Report, Part III,* June 30, 1998; p. 57-58. "Look, I don't understand this," [she] said to Lindsey, "I've been loyal. I have worked through these horrible investigations ... I don't understand why all of a sudden I'm not considered of any value. What has changed?' And [Lindsey] said, 'Look, nothing's changed. You are valued....' My feeling was that for some reason I was not thought to be 'on the team,' which is a phrase you hear a lot and I had not at that point done anything not to be on the team."

[17] Linda Tripp, Larry King Live, *CNN,* February 16, 1999.

[18] Paul W. Valentine, "Maryland Jury to Probe Tripp's taping," *Washington Post,* July 8, 1998; p. A14; access online at: http://www.washingtonpost.com/wp-srv/politics/special/clinton/stories/tripp070898.htm.Also see: "Democrats Pushed for Tripp Wiretap Probe, Lawyers Say," *Associated Press,* July 10, 1998; access online at: http://articles.latimes.com/1998/jul/10/news/mn-2505

[19] *The Columbia Encyclopedia,* Sixth Edition, 2001. Also see: Helen Kennedy, "Md Prosecutors Drop Tripp Wiretapping Charges," *New York Daily News,* May 25, 2000; access online at: http://articles.nydailynews.com/2000-05-25/news/18140068_1_book-agent-lucianne-goldberg-linda-tripp-stephen-montanarelli

[20] Peter J. Boyer, "Life After Vince," *The New Yorker Magazine*, September 11, 1995; access online at: http://www.newyorker.com/archive/1995/09/11/1995_09_11_054_TNY_CARDS_000372740

[21] Hillary Clinton, *Living History,* (First Scribner trade paperback edition 2004), p. 80.

[22] Hillary Clinton, *Living History,* (First Scribner trade paperback

edition 2004), p. 79.

[23] Bill Clinton, *My Life*, (Alfred A. Knopf, 2004), p.530.

[24] Hillary Clinton, *Living History*, (First Scribner trade paperback edition 2004), p. 79.

[25] George Stephanopoulos, *All Too Human*, (Little Brown and Company, 1999) p. 187.

[26] Linda Tripp, *Starr Report, Part III*, p. 4276. See: July 28, 1998, p. 47.

[27] Marinka Peschmann, *The Whistleblower: How the Clinton White House Stayed in Power to Reemerge in the Obama White House and on the World Stage*, (One Rock Ink Publishing, 2012), p. 62. Also see: p. 65-66.

[28] "Tripp's Life Threatened, attorney says," *The Atlanta Journal and Constitution*, May 27, 1998; p. 12a. "Asked whether Tripp was taken to a safe house after the allegations surfaced, Zaccagnini said, "Linda Tripp ... was the subject of a lot of press scrutiny and there were some threats made against her life. As a result, the FBI, in conjunction with Starr's office, decided to move her to a secure location." Also see: "Linda Tripp on Life after the Pentagon," *ABC News/Good Morning America*, February 21, 2001; access online at: http://abcnews.go.com/GMA/story?id=127230&page=1. "Tripp was fired by the Pentagon Jan. 19 after she refused to resign with the other political appointees."

[29] Tony Snow, "Linda Tripp's Comments," *Creators Syndicate*, July 31, 1998. "And now, she feels free to recount some of the things she has seen. She says she was shaken by White House dishonesty during investigations of Vince Foster's death, Filegate, Travelgate and reports of drug abuse among administration employees. "It's chilling," she says, "to watch high government officials lie under oath." ... Tripp made her choice. "There are no standards in that White House," she says, "and I'm not going to be a part of it. I'm going to expose it.""

[30] Marinka Peschmann, *The Whistleblower: How the Clinton White House Stayed in Power to Reemerge in the Obama White House and on the World Stage*, (One Rock Ink Publishing, 2012), p.10- 11. "In 1994, Paula Corbin Jones, a former Arkansas state employee, filed suit against President Clinton. She alleged that when he was the governor of Arkansas, he had propositioned and exposed himself to her in a Little Rock hotel room three years earlier. The whole sordid story was the talk of the nation and the world. Corbin accurately described "distinguishing characteristics" in Clinton's genital area." Also see: Paula Jones Complaint Against President Clinton & Danny Ferguson, filed May 6, 1994; access online at: http://www.lectlaw.com/files/cas03.htm.

## Chapter 2: The Last Day

[31] Bernie Nussbaum, Mark Curriden, *ABA Journal*, March 2, 2009.

[32] Bill Clinton, *Larry King Live*, July 20, 1993. Also see: Bill Clinton, *My Life*, (Alfred A. Knopf, 2004), p. 530.

[33] "Travel Office Legal Fees Total $500,000.00," *Los Angeles Times*, February 16, 1997. "The Treasury "Department has paid about $500,000 in legal fees for seven former White House travel office employees who were fired four years ago. The biggest chunk of the money, $410,607, went to attorneys for Billy R. Dale, the former travel office director who was acquitted of embezzlement charges …'We hope this concludes the long ordeal that the federal government chose to put Billy Dale through,' his attorney said."

[34] What's the Rush? Review & Outlook, *Wall Street Journal*, July 20, 1993.

[35] Chris Ruddy, "Ex-Chief: Politics Kept FBI Off Foster Case," *New York Post*, February 3, 1994.

[36] *White House Press Office*, July 20, 1993.

[37] Bill Clinton, *My Life*, (Alfred A. Knopf, 2004), p. 530.

38 Remarks by the President in Nomination of Judge Louis Freeh, *White House Press* Release, July 20, 1993.

39 *White House Press Briefing,* Updated: November 24, 1993. Also see: Mark Gearan, *White House Press briefing,* August 10, 1993.

40 Kenneth W. Starr, Independent Counsel, *Report on the Death of Vincent W. Foster,* October 10, 1997, p. 30, USPP Report (Morrissette), Dr. Beyer autopsy. See: *Whitewater: The Foster Report,* October 10, 1997; access online via *Washington Post* at: http://www.washingtonpost.com/wp-srv/politics/special/whitewater/docs/foster.htm.

41 Robert B. Fiske, Jr., Special Prosecutor, *Fiske Report,* June 30, 1994, p. 27.

42 *White House Press Briefing,* July 21, 1993; access online at: http://clinton6.nara.gov/1993/07/1993-07-21-press-briefing-on-death-of-vince-foster.html.

43 *White House Press Briefing,* July 21, 1993.

44 *White House Press Briefing,* July 21, 1993. "Q: And no one tried to page him or no attempt to reach him? MR. GEARAN: No. "

45 Betsy Pond, *Park Police Interview,* July 22, 1993, "[Pond] paged Vincent and left the White House number for him to call."

46 Kenneth W. Starr, Independent Counsel, *Report on the Death of Vincent W. Foster,* October 10, 1997, p.72 [209] Rolla OIC 2/9/95, at 27. Investigator Braun 302. 2/7/95, at 8.

47 Kenneth W. Starr, Independent Counsel, *Report on the Death of Vincent W. Foster,* October 10, 1997, p. 72 [208] USPP Evidence /Property Control Receipt (Rolla) at 1-2.

48 Kenneth W. Starr, Independent Counsel, *Report on the Death of Vincent W. Foster,* October 10, 1997, p.72 [210] OIC Doc. No. DC-210-2620. Also see: Kenneth W. Starr, Independent Counsel, *Report on the Death of Vincent W. Foster,* October 10, 1997, p.93.

[49] Progress of the investigation into Whitewater Development Corporation and Related Matters and Recommendations for Future Funding Report, *Senate Whitewater Committee*, 104-204, p.11.

[50] Ruth Marcus (Mike Isikoff staff writer contributed), "Clinton Nominates Reno at Justice," *Washington Post*, February 12, 1993, p.A01; access online at: http://www.washingtonpost.com/wp-srv/politics/govt/admin/stories/reno021293.htm. "In December, Clinton nominated corporate lawyer Zoe E. Baird, who was forced to withdraw because she had violated immigration and tax laws in hiring illegal immigrants. He was poised to name federal judge Kimba M. Wood before she withdrew last week after the disclosure that she had also employed an illegal immigrant to care for her child." Also see: "Nominees, problems with hired help," *Associated Press,* January 9, 2001.

[51] Robert B. Fiske Jr., Special Prosecutor, *Fiske Report,* June 30, 1994, p. 9.

[52] Robert B. Fiske Jr., Special Prosecutor, *Fiske Report,* June 30, 1994, p. 31.

[53] Hillary Clinton, *Living History*, (First Scribner Trade paperback edition, 2004) p. 175.

[54] Hillary Clinton, *Living History*, (First Scribner trade paperback edition 2004), p. 163.

[55] Bill Clinton, *White House Press Briefing,* July 21, 1993.

**Chapter 3: The Foster Investigations**

[56] Hillary Clinton, *Living History*, (First Scribner trade paperback edition 2004), p. 219.

[57] Hillary Clinton, *Living History*, (First Schibner, Trade paperback edition, 2004) p. 297.

[58] *White House Press Briefing,* July 22, 1993.

[59] *White House Press Briefing,* July 22, 1993.

[60] Michael Isikoff, "Park Police to Conduct Inquiry 'Routine' Probe Set on Foster's Death," *Washington Post,* July 27, 1993.

[61] Robert W. Ray, Independent Counsel, *Final Report of the Independent Counsel Re: Madison Guaranty Savings & Loan Association,* January 5, 2001. See: The Clintons, the McDougals, and the Whitewater Development Company, p. 1.

[62] Michael Haddigan, "Susan McDougal Gets 2 Years for Fraud Tied to Whitewater," *Washington Post,* August 21, 1996, p. A14; access online at: http://www.washingtonpost.com/wp-srv/politics/special/whitewater/stories/wwtr960821.htm.

[63] Kenneth W. Starr, Independent Counsel, *Report on the Death of Vincent W. Foster,* October 10, 1997, p. 7 [11] Summary Report by William F. Clinger (Aug. 12, 1994) at 6.

[64] Whitewater Timeline, *CNN*; access online at: http://www.cnn.com/ALLPOLITICS/1997/gen/resources/infocus/whitewater/timeline2.html.

[65] David Lauter, "Clinton's Counsel Nussbaum Resigns," *Los Angeles Times,* March 6, 1994; access online at: http://articles.latimes.com/1994-03-06/news/mn-30792_1_white-house-staff. "White House Counsel Bernard Nussbaum resigned Saturday, bringing to an end a yearlong tenure marked by controversy and accusations that his zealous advocacy of Bill Clinton's interests had compromised the President's political standing."

[66] Susan Schmidt, "Starr Brings Third Indictment Against Hubbell," *Washington Post,* November 14, 1998; p. A1. Also see: Susan Schmidt, "Indictment Claims Hubbells Lived Lavishly," *Washington Post,* May 1, 1998; p.A01; access online: http://www.washingtonpost.com/wp-srv/politics/special/clinton/stories/hubbell050198.htm.

[67] *Report of the Committee on Banking, Housing, and Urban Affairs United States Senate on the Inquiry into the U.S. Park Police Investigation*

*of the Death of White House Deputy Counsel Vincent W. Foster, Jr.,*
Rept. 103-433, Vol. I, January 3, 1995; access online at:
http://www.allanfavish.com/senrep.pdf.

[68] Kenneth W. Starr, Independent Counsel, *Report on the Death of Vincent W. Foster*, October 10, 1997, p. 44.

[69] Robert B. Fiske, Jr., Special Prosecutor, *Fiske Preliminary Report*, June 30, 1994, p.33.

[70] Kenneth W. Starr, Independent Counsel, *Report on the Death of Vincent W. Foster*, October 10, 1997, p. 44.

[71] Kenneth W. Starr, Independent Counsel, *Report on the Death of Vincent W. Foster*, October 10, 1997, p. 75 [221] OIC, 2/16/95, at 17.

[72] Kenneth W. Starr, Independent Counsel, *Report on the Death of Vincent W. Foster*, October 10, 1997, p. 14, Lee Report at 485.

[73] Kenneth W. Starr, Independent Counsel, *Report on the Death of Vincent W. Foster*, October 10, 1997, p.71 [206] .

[74] Robert B. Fiske, Jr., Special Prosecutor, *Fiske Report*, June 30, 1994, p. 48.

[75] Starr Report, *Starr Referral, Supplemental Materials, Part III*, September 28, 1998, p. 4276. "It became very important for the Clintons for their version of the events to be the accepted version of events."

[76] Bill Clinton, *My Life*, (Alfred A. Knopf, 2004), p. 606.

[77] Bill Clinton, *My Life*, (Alfred A. Knopf, 2004), p. 640.

[78] Hillary Clinton, *Living History*, (First Scribner Trade paperback edition, 2004), p. 244.

[79] Hillary Clinton, *Living History*, (First Schibner, Trade paperback edition, 2004), p. 439.

[80] *Final Report of Special Committee to Investigate Whitewater*, January 22, 1996, p. 97-98.

[81] *Final Report of Senate Whitewater Investigation*, June 13, 1996, p.9; access online at: http://www.washingtonpost.com/wp-srv/politics/special/whitewater/committee.pdf.

[82] *Colombia* encyclopedia.

[83] *NYPD Panel on Central Park Jogger Case Issues Report*, January 27, 2003.

[84] Michael Martinez and Brad Johnson, "RFK assassination witness tells CNN there was a second shooter," *CNN*, April 30, 2012; access online:
http://www.cnn.com/2012/04/28/justice/california-rfk-second-gun/?hpt=hp_c2.

[85] "Starr Rules Out Foul Play in Foster Death," *CNN*, February 23, 1997; access online at: http://articles.cnn.com/1997-02-23/politics/starr.report_1_play-in-foster-death-robert-fiske-first-lady?_s=PM:ALLPOLITICS.

## Chapter 4: Rigor Mortis

[86] Robert B. Fiske Jr., Special Prosecutor, *Fiske Report*, June 30, 1994, p. 3.

[87] *National Oceanic and Atmospheric Administration*, (NOAA National Data) July 20, 1993.

[88] Robert B. Fiske Jr., Special Prosecutor, *Fiske Report*, June 30, 1994, p. 30.

[89] Robert B. Fiske Jr., Special Prosecutor, *Fiske Report*, June 30, 1994, p.30.

[90] CW (Confidential Witness), *WABC's John and Paul Alexander Radio Show on The Strange Death of Vince Foster*, July 14, 2001.

[91] Robert B. Fiske Jr., Special Prosecutor, *Fiske Report*, June 30,

---

1994, p.30.

[92] CW (Confidential Witness), *WABC's John and Paul Alexander Radio Show on The Strange Death of Vince Foster*, July 14, 2001.

[93] *Fiske Report*, June 30, 1994, p. 31.

[94] CW (Confidential Witness), *WABC's John Bachelor and Paul Alexander Radio Show on The Strange Death of Vince Foster*, July 14, 2001.

[95] CW (Confidential Witness), WABC's John Bachelor and Paul Alexander Radio Show on The Strange Death of Vince Foster, July 14, 2001.

[96] Robert B. Fiske Jr., Special Prosecutor, *Fiske Report*, June 30, 1994, p. 31 & Starr Report.

[97] Robert B. Fiske Jr., Special Prosecutor, *Fiske Report*, June 30, 1994, p. 31.

[98] Robert B. Fiske Jr., Special Prosecutor, *Fiske Report*, June 30, 1994, p.34.

[99] The Columbia Electronic Encyclopedia, Sixth Edition, *Columbia University Press*. Copyright © 2003.

[100] Kenneth W. Starr, Independent Counsel, *Report on the Death of Vincent W. Foster*, October 10, 1997, p.30.

[101] National Oceanic and Atmospheric Administration (NOAA National Data Center), July 20, 1993.

[102] Peter J. Boyer, "Life After Vince," *The New Yorker Magazine*, September 11, 1995; access online at: http://www.newyorker.com/archive/1995/09/11/1995_09_11_054_TNY_CARDS_000372740.

[103] John Rolla, *U.S. Park Police Report*, July 20, 1993.

[104] Associate Attorney General *Webster Hubbell*, FBI interview,

April 13 and 15, 1994.

[105] Webster Hubbell, *Report of FBI interview*, April 13 & 15, 1994.

[106] *ABC's Nightline, & PBS's Frontline*: Interview with Dee Dee Myers, December 25, 2000.

[107] Bill Clinton, *My Life*, (Alfred A. Knopf, 2004), p.531.

[108] John Rolla, *Deposition of Park Police investigator*, July 21, 1994.

[109] Bill Clinton, *White House Press Briefing*. July 21, 1993.

[110] *White House Press Briefing*, July 22, 1993.

[111] Bernie Nussbaum, 302, 6/8/95 at 6, Ken Starr *Report on the Death of Vincent W. Foster*, October 10, 1997, p. 108.

[112] Kenneth W. Starr, Independent Counsel, *Report on the Death of Vincent W. Foster*, October 10, 1997, p.108. Also see: Douglas Jehl, "Clinton Aide Appeared Depressed Before Death, his Associates Say,' *New York Times*, July 29, 1993; access online at: http://www.nytimes.com/1993/07/29/us/clinton-aide-appeared-depressed-before-death-his-associates-say.html.

[113] Cheryl Braun testimony, *Senate Whitewater Committee*, 1995.

[114] George Lardner Jr. and Susan Schmidt, "Livingstone Resigns, Denying Ill Intent," *Washington Post*, June 27, 1996; Page A01; access online at: http://www.washingtonpost.com/wp-srv/politics/special/whitewater/stories/wwtr960627.htm "Rep. William F. Clinger Jr. (R-Pa.), the committee chairman, opened the hearing by asking why the president would allow "a political operative with a dubious background" and "a total lack of experience" to undertake such a sensitive job."

[115] Bernard Nussbaum *deposition*, Civil No. 96-2123, Washington, D.C., June 4, 1999, p. 24.

[116] *Final Report of the Special Committee to Investigate Whitewater Development Corporation and Related Matters*, June 13, 1996, p. 51;

access online at: http://www.washingtonpost.com/wp-srv/politics/special/whitewater/committee.pdf. Also see: Nussbaum testimony.

[117] *Final Report of the Special Committee to Investigate Whitewater Development Corporation and Related Matters,* June 13, 1996, p. 14; access online at: http://www.washingtonpost.com/wp-srv/politics/special/whitewater/committee.pdf.

[118] Maggie Williams testimony, *Senate Whitewater Committee,* July 25, 1995.

[119] Johnny Chung interview with *NBC's* Tom Brokaw, March 4, 1997. Also see: Charles R. Smith, "The Clinton-China Connection," *Newsmax,* August 9, 2007; access online at: http://archive.newsmax.com/archives/articles/2007/8/8/1521 30.shtml. "In response, Chung handed a $50,000 check to Maggie Williams, Hillary Clinton's chief of staff. On March 11, 1995, Chung and Zheng attended Clinton's weekly radio address, which was later followed by a photo session. Chung later noted that the money came directly from the hands of Gen. Ji, then head of the PLA military intelligence department. Ji handed the money to Chung with the famous words," We like your president (Clinton). We want him re-elected." Still, Mrs. Clinton has a few of her own pictures to live down, including one with convicted "Chinagate" figure Moctar Riady. Yet, the many pictures of Hillary with the Riady family never made it into her "tell-all" book because that family photo series ties her at the hips with Beijing. The Riady family is a direct link to the Chinese army. According to a U.S. Senate report, Moctar and his billion dollar company the Lippo Group, was directly in business with the Chinese military intelligence. Of course, if you ask Hillary, she has never heard of the Riady family."

[120] Hillary Clinton, *Living History,* (First Scribner Trade paperback edition, 2004), p. 391.

[121] Ben Smith, "Clinton Campaign Manager Out," *Politico.com,* February 10, 2008; access online at: http://www.politico.com/blogs/bensmith/0208/Clinton_camp

aign_manager_out.html.

[122] *Final Report of the Special Committee to Investigate Whitewater Development Corporation and Related Matters,* June 13, 1996, p. 9; access online at: http://www.washingtonpost.com/wp-srv/politics/special/whitewater/committee.pdf. "This pattern of concealment and obstruction continues even to the present day. The Special Committee concludes that senior White House officials and other close Clinton associates were not candid in their testimony before the Committee. Specifically, the Committee concludes that Margaret Williams, Chief of Staff to the First Lady, Susan Thomases, a New York attorney and close advisor to Mrs. Clinton, Bernard Nussbaum, then-White House Counsel, and Webster Hubbell, former Associate Attorney General and now-convicted felon, all provided inaccurate and incomplete testimony to the Committee in order to conceal Mrs. Clinton's pivotal role in the decisions surrounding the handling of Mr. Foster's documents following his death ..." Also see: p 14 : "The evidence before the Special Committee established that White House officials engaged in a pattern of deliberate obstruction, and interference with, efforts by law enforcement authorities to conduct their several investigations into Mr. Foster's death. This White House interference began immediately following Mr. Foster's death on the night of July 20. Senior White House officials ignored specific requests by the Park Police to seal Mr. Foster's office on the night of his death. Instead, White House Counsel Bernard Nussbaum, Chief of Staff to the First Lady Margaret Williams and Deputy Assistant to the President Patsy Thomasson entered Mr. Foster's office purportedly to search for a suicide note ..."

[123] Bernard Nussbaum testimony, August 9, 1995. *Final Report of Senate Whitewater Investigation,* June 13, 1996, no 104-280, 52. Also see: David Johnston and Neil A. Lewis, "Report suggests Clinton Counsel Hampered Suicide Investigation," *New York Times,* February 4, 1994; access online at: http://www.nytimes.com/1994/02/04/us/report-suggests-clinton-counsel-hampered-suicide-investigation.html?pagewanted=all&src=pm. "The report also notes that Mr. Nussbaum, along with Patsy Thomasson, a White

House administrative aide and a long-time Clinton associate, and Margaret Williams, Hillary Rodham Clinton's chief of staff, entered and left the office between 10 P.M. and midnight on the night of Mr. Foster's death. Mr. Nussbaum said the three entered the office looking for a suicide note, but did not find one and left after 10 minutes. Mr. Nussbaum said that none of the three removed any documents, but the failure to immediately seal off the office and the unsupervised visit left open the question of whether any of the contents were taken or disturbed." Also see: *Final Report of the Special Committee to Investigate Whitewater Development Corporation and Related Matters,* June 13, 1996, p. 20, access online at: http://www.washingtonpost.com/wp-srv/politics/special/whitewater/committee.pdf. "The Special Committee concludes that its effort to find the truth about the events of July 20–27, 1993 was impeded by what appeared to be a disturbing pattern of incomplete and inaccurate testimony by senior White House officials and close Clinton associates."

[124] Linda Tripp, *Larry King Live*, February 16, 1999.

[125] "The President under Fire;" excerpts from interview with Hillary Clinton on *NBC's Today Show*, January 28, 1998; access online at: http://www.nytimes.com/1998/01/28/us/the-president-under-fire-excerpts-from-interview-with-mrs-clinton-on-nbc.html.

[126] Al Kamen, "Clinton-era Filegate appears to have closed, 14 years on," *Washington Post,* March 10, 2010; access online at: http://www.washingtonpost.com/wp-dyn/content/article/2010/03/09/AR2010030903915.html.

[127] *White House Press Briefing,* July 20, 1993; access online at:http://clinton6.nara.gov/1993/07/1993-07-20-white-house-statement-on-death-of-vince-foster.html.

[128] Bill Clinton, *White House Press Briefing,* July 21, 1993, 12:50 p.m.; access online at: http://clinton6.nara.gov/1993/07/1993-07-21-remarks-on-the-death-of-vince-foster.html.

[129] Chief of Staff Mack McLarty, *White House Press Briefing*, July 21, 1993.

[130] Dee Dee Myers, *White House Press Briefing*, July 22, 1993; access online at: http://clinton6.nara.gov/1993/07/1993-07-22-press-briefing-by-dee-dee-myers.html.

[131] George Stephanopoulos, *All Too Human*, (Little Brown and Company, 1999), p. 185.

[132] Kenneth W. Starr, Independent Counsel, *Report on the Death of Vincent W. Foster*, October 10, 1997, p. 4.

[133] Sally Bedell Smith "The man who knew too much? The truth about the death of Hillary Clinton's close friend Vince Foster," *Daily Mail (UK)*, January 15, 2008; access online at: http://www.dailymail.co.uk/news/article-508210/The-man-knew-The-truth-death-Hillary-Clintons-close-friend-Vince-Foster.html

[134] Larry Brickman, "Foster's Paper: What Executive Privilege?" *New York Times*, August 2, 1995; access online at: http://www.nytimes.com/1995/08/02/opinion/foster-s-papers-what-executive-privilege.html.

[135] "The Last Days of Vince Foster," *Time Magazine*, March 18, 1996; access online at: http://www.time.com/time/magazine/article/0,9171,984262,00.html.

[136] Sally Bedell Smith "The man who knew too much? The truth about the death of Hillary Clinton's close friend Vince Foster," *Daily Mail (UK)*, January 15, 2008; access online at: http://www.dailymail.co.uk/news/article-508210/The-man-knew-The-truth-death-Hillary-Clintons-close-friend-Vince-Foster.html

[137] Kenneth W. Starr, Independent Counsel, *Report on the Death of Vincent W. Foster*, October 10, 1997, p. 109 Lisa Foster interview

[345].

[138] Jason DeParle, "A Life Undone; Portrait of a White House Aide Ensnared by His Perfectionism," *New York Times*, August 22, 1993; access online at: http://www.nytimes.com/1993/08/22/us/life-undone-special-report-portrait-white-house-aide-ensnared-his-perfectionism.html?pagewanted=1.

[139] Hillary Clinton, *Living History*, (First Scribner Trade paperback edition, 2004), p. 390-391.

[140] Bill Clinton, *My Life*, (Alfred A. Knopf, 2004), p. 531.

[141] Hillary Clinton, *Living History*, (First Scribner Trade paperback edition, 2004), p. 174.

## Chapter 6: Inside Hillary's White House Counsel's Office

[142] *Special Committee to Investigate Whitewater*, January 22, 1996, p. 3.

[143] *White House Press Briefing*, July 20, 1993.

[144] *White House Press Briefing*, July 21, 1993.

[145] Kenneth W. Starr, Independent Counsel, *Report on the Death of Vincent W. Foster*, October 10, 1997, p. 74, OIC Doc. No. DC-108-13.

[146] Kenneth W. Starr, Independent Counsel, *Report on the Death of Vincent W. Foster*, October 10, 1997, p. 91.

[147] George Stephanopoulos, *All Too Human*, (Little Brown and Company, 1999), p.184.

[148] Senate Testimony, Henry P. O'Neil, Secret Service Agent, *Special Committee to Investigate Whitewater*, July 27, 1995. Also see: Stephen Labaton, "2 Conflicting Accounts on Files from White House Aide's Office," *New York Times*, July 27, 1995; access online at: http://www.nytimes.com/1995/07/27/us/2-conflicting-accounts-on-files-from-white-house-aide-s-

office.html. "A Secret Service officer today flatly contradicted the White House account of the night of Vincent W. Foster Jr.'s death, telling the Senate Whitewater panel that he had seen Hillary Rodham Clinton's top aide remove files from Mr. Foster's office. The aide vehemently denied doing it. Testifying under oath before the special Senate committee investigating Whitewater, the officer, Henry P. O'Neill, said that on July 20, 1993, several hours after Mr. Foster's body was found in a Virginia park, he saw Mrs. Clinton's chief of staff, Margaret A. Williams, carrying two handfuls of folders from Mr. Foster's office. Miss Williams, who testified that she had gone to the White House that night after being called twice by the First Lady, said she had been drawn to a light in office of Mr. Foster, the deputy White House counsel, in the irrational hope that she would find her colleague still alive there."

[149] Hillary Clinton, *Living History*, (First Scribner Trade paperback edition, 2004), p. 178.

[150] Interview with Dee Dee Myers, *ABC Nightline & PBS's Frontline*, December 2000; access online at: http://www.pbs.org/wgbh/pages/frontline/shows/clinton/interviews/myers3.html.

[151] David Johnston and Neil A. Lewis, "Report Suggests Clinton Counsel Hampered Suicide Investigation," *New York Times*, February 4, 1994; access online at: http://www.nytimes.com/1994/02/04/us/report-suggests-clinton-counsel-hampered-suicide-investigation.html?pagewanted=all&src=pm. "The next morning, Betsy L. Pond, Mr. Nussbaum's secretary, entered the office, straightening papers on Mr. Foster's desk. Secret Service agents arrived at midmorning and did not permit anyone to enter the office, including the park police investigators. Discouraging Candor?"

[152] William Safire, Essay; Foster's Ghosts," *New York Times*, January 6, 1994; access online at: http://www.nytimes.com/1994/01/06/opinion/essay-foster-s-ghost.html.

[153] Nussbaum deposition, *Judicial Watch, Filegate,* Civil No. 96-2123, Washington D.C., June 4, 1999, p. 248.

[154] Andrew Morton, *Monica's Story,* (St. Martin's Press, 1999), p.93.

[155] Hillary Clinton, *Living History,* (First Scribner Trade paperback edition, 2004), p.176.

[156] Stephen Labaton, "Advisers to Mrs. Clinton Are Questioned Anew in Foster Case," *New York Times,* November 3, 1995; access online at:
http://www.nytimes.com/1995/11/03/us/advisers-to-mrs-clinton-are-questioned-anew-in-foster-case.html. "Among the evidence that suggests Mrs. Clinton's involvement in the decision to keep the investigators at bay is the deposition of Stephen R. Neuwirth, an associate White House counsel. He told the committee that he had heard that Ms. Thomases and Mrs. Clinton "may have been concerned about anyone having unfettered access to Mr. Foster's office." Today, Miss Williams was unable to explain several calls that the new records show her making. She offered conflicting testimony about whether she spent the entire morning of July 22, shortly before Mr. Foster's office was searched, at her home or at the White House. Her whereabouts are important for trying to understand why there were calls to Mrs. Clinton in Arkansas that were charged to Miss Williams's home telephone account when she had indicated in earlier testimony that she was in the White House that morning. Ms. Thomases could not explain with precision a series of telephone calls to the White House and to Mrs. Clinton. Her explanations occasionally collided with her earlier testimony. For instance, she testified last summer that she had not decided not to attend Mr. Foster's funeral until late on July 22. But today she said she had told Mrs. Clinton she would not be attending the funeral in a call she received from the First Lady in Little Rock very early on the 22d.

[157] *Special Committee to Investigate Whitewater,* January 22, 1996, p. 11.

[158] Hillary Clinton, *Living History,* (First Scribner Trade paperback edition, 2004), p. 176.

[159] *Final Report of the Special Committee to Investigate Whitewater Development Corporation and Related Matters,* June 13, 1996, p. 57.

[160] Stephen Labaton, "Clinton Aide Removed Files About Legal Work on S & L," *New York Times,* December 12, 1995; access online at: http://www.nytimes.com/1995/12/12/us/clinton-aide-removed-files-about-legal-work-on-s-l.html. "In other action before the committee today, Mrs. Clinton's chief of staff, Margaret A. Williams, provided testimony that conflicted at several points with a former Clinton lawyer, Robert Barnett, about the handling of Mr. Foster's files after his death. This was Miss Williams's third appearance before the committee to discuss Mr. Foster's files and, as in her previous appearances, she was sharply criticized by some Republicans on the committee. Senator Lauch Faircloth, Republican of North Carolina, called Miss Williams a liar and demanded that she step down. "I personally think she should resign from the White House and it is an affront to this committee that she has not," Mr. Faircloth said. But Miss Williams held her ground. At one point she asserted: "I serve at the pleasure of the President. I do not intend to resign until I decide to resign. Further discussion of this serves no real purpose."

[161] *Special Committee to Investigate Whitewater,* January 22, 1996, p. 11, Castleton, 6/27/95 Dep. p.139-140.

[162] Sally Bedell Smith, "Why Hillary Clinton let husband Bill seduce any woman in sight," Extracted from *The Love of Politics: Bill and Hillary Clinton: The White House Years,* (Random House, 2007); access online at: http://www.dailymail.co.uk/femail/article-507762/Why-Hillary-Clinton-let-husband-Bill-seduce-woman-sight.html.

[163] Sally Bedell Smith, *For Love of Politics: Bill and Hillary Clinton: The White House Years,* (Random House, 2007), p. 90. See: From: Source notes, "almost whistling as he whipped through papers," David Gergen, p. 274.

[164] *Special Committee to Investigate Whitewater*, January 22, 1996.

[165] *Special Committee to Investigate Whitewater*, January 22, 1996, p. 3.

[166] Dee Dee Myers, *White House Press Briefing*, July 22, 1993. Also see: Larry Brickman, "Foster's Paper: What Executive Privilege?" *New York Times*, August 2, 1995; access online at: http://www.nytimes.com/1995/08/02/opinion/foster-s-papers-what-executive-privilege.html. "Insofar as the Foster files concerned President Clinton's personal legal and financial matters, they are far outside the scope of executive privilege. Since these papers did not involve the operation of the Executive Office of the President, law enforcement officials were entitled to see them."

[167] Clinton White House Press Briefing, July 22, 1993; access online at: http://clinton6.nara.gov/1993/07/1993-07-22-press-briefing-by-dee-dee-myers.html.

[168] The Watergate Story Timeline, *Washington Post;* access online at: http://www.washingtonpost.com/wp-srv/politics/special/watergate/timeline.html.

[169] Meredith Jessup, "What is executive privilege and what does it mean for F&F investigation? *The Blaze*, June 20, 2012; access online at: http://www.theblaze.com/blog/2012/06/20/what-is-executive-privilege-and-what-does-it-mean-for-ff-investigation/.

[170] *White House Press Briefing*, July 22, 1993.

## Chapter 7: Jeopardy

[171] *Code of Ethics for U.S. Government Service*, adopted July 11, 1958; access online at: http://usgovinfo.about.com/blethics.htm.

[172] Mark Gearan, *White House Press Briefing*, July 21, 1993.

[173] Bill Clinton, Remarks by the President, *The White House Rose Garden*, July 21, 1993.

## Chapter 8: You Are Not Going To Get Much

[174] Sally Bedell Smith, "Why Hillary Clinton let husband Bill seduce any woman in sight," Extracted from: *The Love of Politics: Bill and Hillary Clinton: The White House Years*, (Random House, 2007).

[175] Marinka Peschmann, *The Whistleblower: How the Clinton White House Stayed in Power to Reemerge in the Obama White House and on the World Stage*, (One Rock Ink Publishing, 2012), p. 62. Also see p. 65-66. Also see: Peter Baker and Susan Schmidt, "Lewinsky Gets Immunity for Her Testimony," *Washington Post*, July 29, 1998. p. A01; access online at: http://www.washingtonpost.com/wp-srv/politics/special/clinton/stories/starr072998.htm. "A White House official said Kendall is seeking to put off Clinton's testimony to force Starr to delay any report on potentially impeachable offenses until after the fall elections and a new Congress convenes in January, and so Clinton will get a chance to learn what Lewinsky says in her testimony. Lawyers for many of the witnesses in Starr's six-month grand jury investigation have participated in a **White House joint defense** agreement under which they share information. While Lewinsky is not part of the joint defense agreement, information at times has flowed easily in back channels from her lawyers to the Clinton team."

[176] Marinka Peschmann, *The Whistleblower: How the Clinton White House Stayed in Power to Reemerge in the Obama White House and on the World Stage*. (One Rock Ink, 2012), p. 58. "Billy Dale was escorted out of the White House by the FBI, put into a paneled van with no seats and told to sit on the floor the day the Clintons removed him. And I watched Hillary orchestrate that whole thing; siccing the FBI on them, getting them out. Careerists, while they're not political, do serve at the pleasure of the president. All President Clinton had to say was, 'We're replacing you.' It would've been unheard of, but was within his legal purview to do." Instead the Clintons did what Linda said they always did: "Destroy their enemy and ruin them." The abrupt travel office firings were triggered by what the Clinton White House claimed were allegations of sloppy accounting. In December 1994, Billy Dale was indicted on two counts of embezzlement. The press went berserk criticizing the new

administration. In its aftermath, five of the staffers were reinstated, and in a self-critical report the White House admitted it "erred and would never again short circuit proper legal channels by bypassing the Justice Department in seeking an FBI investigation." Also listen to online *Whistleblower* audio accompaniment #1; access online at:

http://www.marinkapeschmann.com/2012/05/07/exclusive-audio-the-vetting-the-clintons-and-the-never-before-heard-tripp-tapes/.

177 Linda Tripp, *Starr Referral, Supplemental Materials, Part III*, Starr Report, September 28, 1998, p. 4237-4237, See July 16, 98, p. 20-21.

178 David Johnston and Neil A. Lewis, "Report Suggests Clinton Counsel Hampered Suicide Investigation," *New York Times*, February 4, 1994. "Mr. Nussbaum directed other lawyers in the White House counsel's office to monitor and take notes while investigators interviewed assistants in the office, potentially inhibiting candor, the report said. At one point, the report said, Mr. Nussbaum burst in on the questioning of Ms. Pond to demand whether anything was wrong."

179 David Johnston and Neil A. Lewis, "Report Suggests Clinton Counsel Hampered Suicide Investigation," *New York Times*, February 4, 1994; access online at:

http://www.nytimes.com/1994/02/04/us/report-suggests-clinton-counsel-hampered-suicide-investigation.html?pagewanted=all&src=pm. "The report says that Mr. Nussbaum interfered with interviews of witnesses by directing that other White House lawyers sit in, the officials said, and that he denied the park police access to documents in the office of the deputy White House counsel, Vincent W. Foster Jr., as the park police looked into his death ... Investigators said Mr. Nussbaum's actions hampered their ability to understand what factors may have motivated Mr. Foster to take his life. For example, the investigators believed that having White House lawyers sit in on interviews with other staff members interfered with the effort to obtain candid statements. Mr. Nussbaum defended that decision as proper."

---

[180] *Final Report of the Special Committee to Investigate Whitewater Development Corporation and Related Matters*, June 13, 1996, p. 15; access online at: http://www.washingtonpost.com/wp-srv/politics/special/whitewater/committee.pdf.

[181] *Final Report of the Special Committee to Investigate Whitewater Development Corporation and Related Matters*, June 13, 1996, p. 64.

[182] Brian Knowlton, "Deal Ends Possibility of Clinton Indictment," *New York Times*, January 20, 2001; access online at: http://www.nytimes.com/2001/01/20/news/20iht-clint.2.t_3.html?pagewanted=all.

Also see: Eric Lichtblau, "Clinton Strikes Indictment deal; Case is dropped as President Admits to False testimony," *Los Angeles Times*, January 20, 2001, Part A, National Desk, p. 1.

[183] Margaret Carlson, *Time Magazine* interview, 1993.

[184] *Final Report of the Special Committee to Investigate Whitewater*, p.105-105. Also see: Christopher Ruddy, *Strange Death of Vince Foster* (Simon & Schuster, 1997), p. 123.

[185] *Special Committee to Investigate Whitewater*, January 22, 1996 p. 3 (Margolis, 8/10/95 Hrg., pp. 182-183). Also see: Stephen Labaton, "Advisers to Mrs. Clinton Are Questioned Anew in Foster Case," *New York Times*, November 3, 1995; access online at: http://www.nytimes.com/1995/11/03/us/advisers-to-mrs-clinton-are-questioned-anew-in-foster-case.html. "Justice Department officials have testified that the White House counsel, Bernard W. Nussbaum, agreed on July 21, 1993, the day after Mr. Foster's death, to let investigators study his files, but he reneged the next day after consulting with other White House officials. Mr. Nussbaum has denied making such an agreement with the department and has asserted that he decided on his own to prevent the investigators from searching Mr. Foster's files for clues about why he killed himself.

[186] Neil A. Lewis, "Top Justice Official Testifies of Limits On Foster Inquiry," *New York Times*, August 11, 1995; access online at: http://www.nytimes.com/1995/08/11/us/top-justice-

official-testifies-of-limits-on-foster-inquiry.html. "Mr. Margolis said Mr. Nussbaum had reneged on an agreement to let Justice Department lawyers view the first pages of files found in Mr. Foster's office for any evidence as to why he might have killed himself, including possible evidence of extortion or blackmail. In his testimony, Mr. Nussbaum vigorously defended his conduct and told the Senators that he had never made such an agreement with Mr. Margolis. Instead, citing the need to protect any privilege or confidentiality for President Clinton and his wife, Hillary, Mr. Nussbaum kept law-enforcement officials at arm's length in Mr. Foster's office while he sat at Mr. Foster's desk and reviewed the documents himself, one by one, deciding which could be turned over to the investigators. In one instance, Mr. Margolis said, Mr. Nussbaum would not let law-enforcement officials in the room even to see a newspaper clipping found in Mr. Foster's files, asserting it was shielded by executive privilege." "He indicated that would be an invasion of the President's deliberative process," Mr. Margolis testified to laughter in the committee hearing room. Mr. Margolis, who was one of two Justice Department officials in the room, said he felt he was being used to dress up the legitimacy of Mr. Nussbaum's search. Mr. Margolis recounted in detail his recollections of a conversation with Mr. Nussbaum about an agreement for Mr. Margolis to review the Foster documents. "I was certain that day, and I am certain now, that there was such an agreement and Mr. Nussbaum was aware of it," he said.

[187] USPP [United States Park Police] *Captain Hume's Foster report* 1993: "At one point Special Agent Scott Salter got up to stretch and Clifford Sloan challenged him and asked him if he was standing up in an attempt to get a look at the documents."

[188] Linda Tripp & Senate Testimony, Scott Salter, *Final Report of Special Committee to Investigate Whitewater*, July 27, 1995, p.72 –73 (Ch. 6 #42).

[189] *Special Committee to Investigate Whitewater*, January 22, 1996, p. 4 (Margolis, 8/10/95 Hrg. P. 191; Salter, 7/27/95 Hrg. p. 105; Adams, 7/27/95 Hrg. P.105; Park Police Document 37).

[190] Neil A. Lewis, "Top Justice Official Testifies of Limits on Foster Inquiry," *New York Times,* August 11, 1995.

[191] *Special Committee to Investigate Whitewater,* January 22, 1996, p. 4 (Heymann, 8/2/95 Hrg. P.53).

[192]*Final Report of the Special Committee to Investigate Whitewater Development Corporation and Related Matters,* June 13, 1996, p. 15 and 21-22; access online at:
http://www.washingtonpost.com/wp-srv/politics/special/whitewater/committee.pdf.

[193] *Final Report of the Special Committee to Investigate Whitewater Development Corporation and Related Matters,* June 13, 1996, p. 17.

[194] Dee Dee Myers, *ABC's Nightline & PBS's Frontline,* December 2000.

[195] Jane Sherburne, "Clinton White House Special Counsel," *ABC's Nightline & PBS's Frontline,* January 2001.

[196] Matt Drudge, "Tripp Turns on Clintons," *Drudge Report,* August 3, 1997; access online at:
http://www.drudgereportarchives.com/dsp/specialReports_pc_carden_detail.htm?reportID=%7BC6F47835-901D-4D27-BB53-37E48E2708FF%7D. Also see: *Final Report of the Special Committee to Investigate Whitewater Development Corporation and Related Matters,* June 13, 1996, p. 74; access online at:
http://www.washingtonpost.com/wp-srv/politics/special/whitewater/committee.pdf.

[197] *White House Press Briefing,* July 22, 1993.

## Chapter 9: Plastic Flowers

[198] Jason DeParle, "President Returns Home to Bury Boyhood Friend," *New York Times,* July 24, 1993; access online at:
http://www.nytimes.com/1993/07/24/us/president-returns-home-to-bury-boyhood-friend.html?scp=23&sq=Vincent%20Foster&st=cse. "Speaking in a cathedral packed with the state's political and legal elite, the

President described Vincent W. Foster Jr., the deputy White House counsel, as a lifelong protector whose failure to protect himself is beyond human understanding."

[199] Wesley Pruden, "Rallying the corpses for the Dems," *Washington Times/ Jewish World Review*, Nov. 1, 2002.

[200] William Saletan, "No Contest – Paul Wellstone's memorial service turns into a pep rally," *Slate*, October 29, 2002; access online at: http://www.slate.com/articles/news_and_politics/ballot_box/2002/10/no_contest.html. "But the solemnity of death and the grace of Midwestern humor are overshadowed tonight by the angry piety of populism. Most of the event feels like a rally. The touching recollections are followed by sharply political speeches urging Wellstone's supporters to channel their grief into electoral victory. The crowd repeatedly stands, stomps, and whoops. The roars escalate each time Walter Mondale, the former vice president who will replace Wellstone on the ballot, appears on the giant screens suspended above the stage. "Fritz! Fritz!" the assembly chants. "Politics is not about winning for the sake of winning," Wellstone declares in a videotaped speech shown on the overhead screens. "Politics is about improving people's lives." But as the evening's speakers proceed, it becomes clear that to them, honoring Wellstone's legacy is all about winning the election. Repeating the words of Wellstone's son, the assembly shouts, "We will win! We will win!" … Somewhere, Wellstone must be turning on his cross."

[201] Vince Foster, Commencement address, *The University of Arkansas Law School* at Fayetteville, Arkansas, May 8, 1993, [*Fiske Report*, p. 17] [Starr. p. 105].

[202] The Encyclopedia of Arkansas History and Culture, *Whitewater Scandal;* access online at: http://encyclopediaofarkansas.net/encyclopedia/entry-detail.aspx?entryID=4061.

[203] *Final Report of Senate Whitewater Investigation*, June 13, 1996, p.9; access online at:

http://www.washingtonpost.com/wp-srv/politics/special/whitewater/committee.pdf.

[204] Michael Haddigan, "Susan McDougal Gets 2 Years for Fraud Tied to Whitewater," *Washington Post,* August 21, 1996, p. A14.

[205] Sonya Ross, "Clinton Pardons More Than 100," *Associated Press,* January 20, 2001. Also see: Susan Schmidt, "James McDougal Dies While Awaiting Parole," *Washington Post,* March 9, 1998.

[206] Gwen Ifill, "White House Aide Found Dead; Close Associate of the Clintons," *New York Times,* July 21, 1993; access online at: http://www.nytimes.com/1993/07/21/obituaries/white-house-aide-found-dead-close-associate-of-the-clintons.html.

[207] Mara Leveritt, "Bloody awful: How money and politics contaminated Arkansas's prison plasma program," *Arkansas Times,* August 16, 2007. Also see: Sarah –Taissir Bencharif, "John Plater, man who fought for tainted blood victims, dead at 45," *Toronto Star,* August 2, 2012; access online at: http://www.thestar.com/news/gta/article/1235674--john-plater-man-who-fought-for-tainted-blood-victims-dead-at-46 Read more from multiple sources on the tainted blood here: http://prorev.com/blood.htm Partial summary. "In the mid-1980s, as contaminated blood flowed from Arkansas inmates to other countries, then-Governor W.J. Clinton sat on his hands despite evidence of severe mismanagement in his prison system and its medical operations. The prison medical program was being run by Health Management Associates, which was headed by Leonard Dunn, a man who would brag to state police of his close ties to Clinton. Some of the killer blood ended up in Canada where it contributed to the deaths of an unknown number of blood and plasma recipients. An estimated 2,000 Canadian recipients of blood and related products got the AIDS virus between 1980 and 1985. At least 60,000 Canadians were infected with the hepatitis C virus between 1980 and 1990. Arkansas was one of the few sources of bad blood during this period. The Royal Canadian Mounted Police has a staff of 24 working on the case. So far, investigators have interviewed about

600 people including in the U.S., Germany and the Netherlands. According to the Ottawa Citizen, the team has more than 30,000 documents. Other Arkansas plasma was sent to Switzerland, Spain, Japan, and Italy. In a case with strong echoes of the Arkansas scandal, a former premier of France and two of his cabinet colleagues are currently on trial stemming from the wrongful handling of blood supplies. Some of the blood in the French controversy may have come from Arkansas. A 1992 Newsday report on the French scandal noted that three persons had been convicted for their role in distributing blood they knew was contaminated: "Throughout the 1980s and later, blood was taken from prison donors for use in blood banks despite a series of directives warning against such a practice. According to the report, donations from prisoners accounted for 25 percent of all the contaminated blood products in France. Blood from prisons was 69 times more contaminated that that of the general population of donors." The Arkansas blood program was also grossly mishandled by the Food and Drug Administration. And the scandal provides yet another insight into how the American media misled the public about Clinton during the 1992 campaign. The media ignored a major Clinton scandal despite, for example, 80 articles about it in the Arkansas Democrat in just one four-month period of the mid-80s."

[208] The Progressive Review. Last updated in 2000. Access online at: http://prorev.com/legacy.htm

[209] Bill Clinton, *My Life*, (Alfred A. Knopf, 2004), p. 532.

[210] George Stephanopoulos, *All Too Human*, (Little Brown and Company, 1999), p. 277 & 278.

[211] Senate Testimony, Stephen Neuwirth, July 10, 1995, "Special Committee to Investigate White Water," *New York Times*, August 4, 1995, See 195.

## Chapter 10: Damage Control

[212] *Final Report of Senate Whitewater Investigation*, June 13, 1996, p.85; access online at:

http://www.washingtonpost.com/wp-
srv/politics/special/whitewater/committee.pdf.

[213] *Special Committee to Investigate Whitewater*, January 22, 1996, p. 4.

[214] David Johnston and Neil A. Lewis, "Report suggests Clinton
Counsel Hampered Suicide Investigation," *New York Times*,
February 4, 1994; access online at:
http://www.nytimes.com/1994/02/04/us/report-suggests-
clinton-counsel-hampered-suicide-
investigation.html?pagewanted=all&src=pm. "The park police
investigators distrusted Mr. Nussbaum's account of the
circumstances surrounding the discovery in Mr. Foster's
briefcase of the note six days after his death, according to the
report. The note, a bitter lament on Washington politics, was
found by Stephen R. Neuwirth, another Nussbaum aide. One
investigator said he had watched Mr. Nussbaum inspect the
briefcase earlier without finding the note. The park police report,
which has not been made public, does not directly accuse Mr.
Nussbaum of wrongdoing. Rather, the officials said, it draws a
harsh picture of the top White House lawyer trying to restrict the
inquiry."

[215] Stephen Labaton, "Former Presidential Counsel cast as
Whitewater's Heavy," *New York Times*, July 31, 1995; access
online at: http://www.nytimes.com/1995/07/31/us/former-
presidential-counsel-cast-as-whitewater-s-heavy.html. "Six days
after the suicide of Vincent W. Foster Jr., Bernard W. Nussbaum
urgently led Hillary Rodham Clinton into his White House
counsel's office. He showed her a note, which had been found in
shreds on the bottom of Mr. Foster's briefcase and lay on his
conference table, pieced together by Mr. Nussbaum and an aide
like a jigsaw puzzle. In it, Mr. Foster, one of Mrs. Clinton's
oldest and dearest friends, spoke of his anguish about
Washington."

[216] David Johnston and Neil A. Lewis, "Report suggests Clinton
Counsel Hampered Suicide Investigation," *New York Times*,
February 4, 1994.

²¹⁷ Senate Testimony, Neuwirth, July 10, 1995, "Special
Committee to Investigate Whitewater," *New York Times,* August
4, 1995, See 195.

²¹⁸ Robert Pear, "White House Memo Deals with Delay in
Surrendering Suicide Note," *New York Times,* August 28, 1996;
access online at:
http://query.nytimes.com/gst/fullpage.html?res=9D01E1DE11
39F93BA1575BC0A960958260.

²¹⁹ R.W. Apple Jr., "Note Left by White House Aide:
Accusation, Anger and Despair," *New York Times,* August 11,
1993; access online at:
http://www.nytimes.com/1993/08/11/us/note-left-by-white-
house-aide-accusation-anger-and-despair.html. "After being
missed in an initial search on July 22, the note was found on July
26, the Justice Department said. But it was not turned over to
investigators by the White House until 30 hours later—a delay
attributed by the White House to the need to let Mr. Foster's
family and the President see the fragments first. Chief Robert E.
Langston of the United States Park Police, which conducted the
initial investigation into the death, said his officers "certainly
weren't pleased" about the delay."

²²⁰ Douglas Jehl, "Notes by Suicide Withheld a Day by White
House," *New York Times,* July 30, 1993; access online at:
http://www.nytimes.com/1993/07/30/us/notes-by-suicide-
withheld-a-day-by-white-house.html. "The White House waited
for about 30 hours before giving Federal investigators the scraps
of a torn-up note found on Monday in the briefcase of Vincent
W. Foster Jr. ... Officials said the White House turned over the
note to Park Police after an internal debate, involving senior
staff members and eventually Attorney General Janet Reno,
produced a consensus that the note should be turned over to
investigators."

²²¹ "Memo Links First Lady To Handling Of Suicide Note,"
*CNN,* August 27, 1996; access online at:
http://www.cnn.com/ALLPOLITICS/1996/news/9608/27/w
hitewater/index.shtml. " ... newly released documents suggest

[Hillary] was behind the 30-hour delay in releasing late White House counsel Vincent Foster's suicide note to authorities. How the White House handled Foster's 1993 death, and the possibility that administration officials improperly removed documents from his office or impeded an official search of it, has been the subject of intense scrutiny by congressional Republicans and the media … That contradicts sworn testimony to the Senate Whitewater Committee from Clinton staffers that the first lady had no role whatsoever in the handling of Foster's note."

[222] Kenneth W. Starr, Independent Counsel, *Report on the Death of Vincent W. Foster*, October 10, 1997, p. 106 [FBI Lab Report, 7/5/95]. Also see: David Johnston, "New Gap Arises in Inquiry into Death of Clinton Aide," *New York Times*, August 14, 1993; access online at: http://www.nytimes.com/1993/08/14/us/new-gap-arises-in-inquiry-into-death-of-clinton-aide.html."A partial but identifiable palm print was found on an anguished note left by Vincent W. Foster Jr., but it has never been investigated, Government officials said today. The disclosure contradicts the assertions of the Federal law-enforcement officials who said this week that only a smudged, unreadable palm print had been found."

[223] David Johnston and Neil A. Lewis, "Report Suggests Clinton Counsel Hampered Investigation," *New York Times*, February 4, 1994. "At that point, the Federal Bureau of Investigation entered the case to determine whether there were any irregularities in the handling of the note. The F.B.I. investigation found no wrongdoing, but its fingerprint analysis uncovered only a partial smudged palm print and no fingerprints on the note. Some investigators said that the lack of fingerprints seemed to suggest that Mr. Foster wrote the note and then tore into 28 pieces without leaving any prints—a circumstance that is not dealt with conclusively in the report."

[224] Foster's "suicide note,' see Starr or Fiske report for image.

[225] Mark Gearan, *White House Press Briefing*, July 20, 1993.

[226] Hillary Clinton, *Living History*, (First Scribner Trade paperback edition, 2004), p. 178.

[227] Linda Tripp, *Starr Referral Supplemental Materials Part III*, September 28, 1998, p. 4276.

## Chapter 11: The Confession and the Case

[228] Law enforcement interview.

[229] The American Heritage Dictionary, Third Edition, *Houghton, Mifflin Company 1992*, p. 400.

[230] Tripp interview, *USPP Report*, 7/22/93, at 1.

[231] Linda Tripp, OIC 6/21/95, at 9, Kenneth W. Starr, Independent Counsel, *Report on the Death of Vincent W. Foster*, October 10, 1997, p.86.

[232] Whitewater: The Foster Report via the *Washington Post, access* online at: http://www.washingtonpost.com/wp-srv/politics/special/whitewater/docs/fosterviii.htm.

[233] Kenneth W. Starr, Independent Counsel, *Report on the Death of Vincent W. Foster*, October 10, 1997, p. 86.

[234] Kenneth W. Starr, Independent Counsel, *Report on the Death of Vincent W. Foster*, October 10, 1997, p. 86, Pond, OIC, 4/26/95, at 9, Castleton, OIC, 4/4/95, at 77.

[235] Kenneth W. Starr, Independent Counsel, *Report on the Death of Vincent W. Foster*, October 10, 1997, p. 90 Patsy Thomasson, OIC, 8/31/94, at 32.

[236] Marinka Peschmann, *The Whistleblower: How the Clinton White House Stayed in Power to Reemerge in the Obama White House and on the World Stage*, (One Rock Ink, 2012), p.65. "President Clinton testified: "My goal in this deposition was to be truthful, but not particularly helpful. I do not wish to do the work of the Jones lawyers…""

[237] Kenneth W. Starr, Independent Counsel, *Report on the Death of Vincent W. Foster*, October 10, 1997, p. 92.

[238] CW (Confidential Witness), *WABC's John and Paul Alexander Radio Show on The Strange Death of Vince Foster*, July 14, 2001.

[239] Deposition: Clifford Bernath, Deputy Assistant Secretary of Defense of Public Affairs, *Civil Action Nos. 96-2123 & 97-1288*, Washington D.C., April 30, 1998, p. 126.

[240] Hillary Clinton, *Living History*, (First Scribner Trade paperback edition, 2004), p. 141.

[241] Kenneth W. Starr, Independent Counsel, *Report on the Death of Vincent W. Foster*, October 10, 1997, p. 44.

[242] Robert B. Fiske Jr., Special Counsel, *Fiske Report*, June 30, 1994, p. 43.

[243] Robert B. Fiske Jr., Special Counsel, *Fiske Report*, FBI Lab Report p. 46.

[244] Kenneth W. Starr, Independent Counsel, *Report on the Death of Vincent W. Foster*, October 10, 1997, p. 55, [154]FBI Lab Report, 5/9/94, at 11; OIC Investigators' Memorandum, 3/2/95, at 4 (Lab Conference)..

[245] Kenneth W. Starr, Independent Counsel, *Report on the Death of Vincent W. Foster*, October 10, 1997, p. 55.

[246] Kenneth W. Starr, Independent Counsel, *Report on the Death of Vincent W. Foster*, October 10, 1997, p. 56.

[247] Robert B. Fiske Jr., Special Counsel, *Fiske Report*, June 30, 1994, p. 40.

[248] "The White House Announces Restorations," *The White House Office of the Press Secretary*, November 24, 1993.

[249] "The White House Announces Restorations," The White House Office of the Press Secretary, November 24, 1993.

250 Vincent J. Scalice, "What really happened," access online at: http://whatreallyhappened.com/content/vince-foster-documents-reveal-judges-deliberations-death.

251 Kenneth W. Starr, Independent Counsel, *Report on the Death of Vincent W. Foster*, October 10, 1997, p. 54.

252 Kenneth W. Starr, Independent Counsel, *Report on the Death of Vincent W. Foster*, October 10, 1997, [149] Lee Report at 492-93.

253 Kenneth W. Starr, Independent Counsel, *Report on the Death of Vincent W. Foster*, October 10, 1997, p. 54.

254 Robert B. Fiske Jr., Special Prosecutor. *Fiske Report*, June 30, 1994, p. 35.

255 Robert B. Fiske Jr., Special Prosecutor, *Fiske Report*, June 30, 1994, p. 56.

256 Robert B. Fiske Jr., Special Prosecutor, *Fiske Report*, June 30, 1994, p. 56.

257 George Stephanopoulos, *All Too Human*, (Little Brown and Company, 1999) p. 112.

258 Kenneth W. Starr, Independent Counsel, *Report on the Death of Vincent W. Foster*, October 10, 1997, p. 58 [167] Lee Report at 422.

259 Robert B. Fiske Jr., Special Prosecutor, *Fiske Report*, June 30, 1994, p. 53.

260 U.S. Park Police Report, Hearings, volume 2, 2123.

261 *FBI Evidence Control Receipt*, 4/2/1994. "Foster's Body; 1: Looking down from top of berm, 2: focusing on face, 3: focusing on Right side shoulder/arm, 4: body taken from below the feet, 5: focusing on right side and arm, 6:focus on top of head, then [sic] heavy foliage, 7; face: looking directing down into face, 8: face; taken from right side focusing on face, blood on shoulder." Also see: Kenneth W. Starr, Independent Counsel,

*Report on the Death of Vincent W. Foster*, October 10, 1997, p.73
[212].

262 Kenneth W. Starr, Independent Counsel, *Report on the Death of
Vincent W. Foster*, October 10, 1997, p.63 [187].

263 Robert B. Fiske Jr., Special Prosecutor, *Fiske Report*, June 30,
1994, p. 33, FBI Lab at 9.

264 Kenneth W. Starr, Independent Counsel, *Report on the Death of
Vincent W. Foster*, October 10, 1997, p.65.

265 Kenneth W. Starr, Independent Counsel, *Report on the Death of
Vincent W. Foster*, October 10, 1997, see Bloodstain Patterns as
Depicted in Photographs from Scene.

266 Kenneth W. Starr, Independent Counsel, *Report on the Death of
Vincent W. Foster*, October 10, 1997, p. 67.

267 Kenneth W. Starr, Independent Counsel, *Report on the Death of
Vincent W. Foster*, October 10, 1997, p. 65 [189] Blackbourne
Report at 4.

268 Kenneth W. Starr, Independent Counsel, *Report on the Death of
Vincent W. Foster*, October 10, 1997, p.64. "Dr. Blackbourne
concluded that the blood draining from the right nostril and
right side of the mouths, as documented by Polaroid scene
photographs, suggests that an early observer may have caused
movement of the head."

269 Robert B. Fiske Jr., Special Prosecutor, *Fiske Report*, June 30,
1994, p. 32.

270 Kenneth W. Starr, Independent Counsel, *Report on the Death of
Vincent W. Foster*, October 10, 1997, p.65 [189].

271 Robert B. Fiske Jr., Special Prosecutor, *Fiske Report*, June 30,
1994, p. 32.

272 Kenneth W. Starr, Independent Counsel, *Report on the Death of
Vincent W. Foster*, October 10, 1997, p.63 [187].

273 Robert B. Fiske Jr., Special Prosecutor, *Fiske Report*, June 30, 1994, p. 53.

274 Kenneth W. Starr, Independent Counsel, *Report on the Death of Vincent W. Foster*, October 10, 1997, p.29 [64] Beyer, OIC, 2/16/95, at 10-11.

275 *Gale Encyclopedia of Surgery: A Guide for Patients and Caregivers* - Copyright 2005 by Thomson Gale, a part of the Thomson Corporation.

276 Kenneth W. Starr, Independent Counsel, *Report on the Death of Vincent W. Foster*, October 10, 1997, Autopsy report, p. 29.

277 Kenneth W. Starr, Independent Counsel, *Report on the Death of Vincent W. Foster*, October 10, 1997, p. 48 [132], OIC Investigators' Memorandum, Lee Report at 492.

278 Kenneth W. Starr, Independent Counsel, *Report on the Death of Vincent W. Foster*, October 10, 1997, p. 50.

279 The Progressive Review.

280 *Special Committee to Investigate Whitewater*, January 22, 1996, p. 11.

281 Hillary Clinton, *Living History*, (First Scribner Trade paperback edition 2004), p. 175.

282Kenneth W. Starr, Independent Counsel, *Report on the Death of Vincent W. Foster*, October 10, 1997, p. 74, [217] Rolla, OIC, 2/9/95 at 35-36; Braun OIC, 2/9/95, at 75-76.

283Kenneth W. Starr, Independent Counsel, *Report on the Death of Vincent W. Foster*, October 10, 1997, p. 74 [217] Rolla, OIC, 2/9/95, at 35-36.

284 Senate Deposition, Braun, Hearings, Volume 1, 501.

285 Kenneth W. Starr, Independent Counsel, *Report on the Death of Vincent W. Foster*, October 10, 1997, p. 72 [208] USPP Evidence/

Property Control receipt (Rolla) at 1-2.

[286] Investigator John Rolla, *Deposition of Park Police*, July 20 and 21, 1994. Also see: *Senate testimony* of Park Police Investigator John Rolla, July 20, 1995.

[287] Kenneth W. Starr, Independent Counsel, *Report on the Death of Vincent W. Foster*, October 10, 1997, p. 27 [56] USPP Report (Smith) at 1.

[288] Kenneth W. Starr, Independent Counsel, *Report on the Death of Vincent W. Foster*, October 10, 1997, p. 56.

[289] Kenneth W. Starr, Independent Counsel, *Report on the Death of Vincent W. Foster*, October 10, 1997, p. 20, [29] & [30].

[290] Kenneth W. Starr, Independent Counsel, *Report on the Death of Vincent W. Foster*, October 10, 1997, p.71 [206].

[291] Robert B. Fiske Jr., Special Prosecutor, *Fiske Report*, June 30, 1994, p. 47.

[292] Kenneth W. Starr, Independent Counsel, *Report on the Death of Vincent W. Foster*, October 10, 1997, p. 32 [67] Officer Morrissett's report & Dr. Beyer @ [69].

[293] Kenneth W. Starr, Independent Counsel, *Report on the Death of Vincent W. Foster*, October 10, 1997, p. 96 [299] 302, 9/12-10/31/95, at 4 (Investigators' Report of Search).

## Chapter 12: The Death of Vince Foster

[294] Kenneth W. Starr, Independent Counsel, *Report on the Death of Vincent W. Foster*, October 10, 1997, Appendix to Report; September 23, 1997 letter from Patrick Knowlton's attorney, John H. Clarke.

[295] Kenneth W. Starr, Independent Counsel, *Report on the Death of Vincent W. Foster*, October 10, 1997, p. 30, USPP Report (Morrissette), Dr. Beyer autopsy. See: *Whitewater: The Foster Report*, October 10, 1997, access online via *Washington Post* at:

http://www.washingtonpost.com/wp-srv/politics/special/whitewater/docs/foster.htm.

296 Kenneth W. Starr, Independent Counsel, *Report on the Death of Vincent W. Foster*, October 10, 1997, p. 36-37.

297 William Safire, "Essay; Vincent Foster's "Can of Worms," *New York Times*, July 24, 1995; access online at: http://www.nytimes.com/1995/07/24/opinion/essay-vincent-foster-s-can-of-worms.html

298 Sally Bedell Smith "The man who knew too much? The truth about the death of Hillary Clinton's close friend Vince Foster," *Daily Mail (UK)*, January 15, 2008; access online at: http://www.dailymail.co.uk/news/article-508210/The-man-knew-The-truth-death-Hillary-Clintons-close-friend-Vince-Foster.html

299 Reed Irvine, *AIM Report*, Witness Jeanne Slade, July 1, 2001, access online at: http://www.aim.org/aim-report/aim-report-evidence-proving-foster-was-murdered/.

300 Kenneth W. Starr, *Independent Counsel, Report on the Death of Vincent W. Foster*, October 10, 1997, p. 56.

301 Kenneth W. Starr, Independent Counsel, *Report on the Death of Vincent W. Foster*, October 10, 1997, p. 47 [127] Lab Report at 9. Also see Part 5: FBI Laboratory: "The contact stain on the right cheek and jaw of the victim is typical of having been caused by a blotting action, such as would happen if a *blood-soaked object was brought in contact with the side of his face and taken away, leaving the observed pattern behind.* The closest blood-bearing object which could have caused this staining is the right shoulder of the victim's shirt. The quantity, configuration and distribution of the blood on the shirt and the right cheek and jaw of the victim are consistent with *the jaw being in contact with the shoulder of the shirt at some time.*" "Dr. Lee also examined the photographs taken at Fort Marcy Park. He noted that the photographs of the shirt show several areas of bloodstains, including "saturated-type

bloodstains" on the "shoulder and collar region."

302 Kenneth W. Starr, Independent Counsel, *Report on the Death of Vincent W. Foster*, October 10, 1997, Dr. Berman, p. 98.

303 Route: Slight right onto Elllipse Rd. NW, left on 16th NW, Right on Constitution Avenue NW/US-50 to GW Parkway Exit, to the Park.

304 Reed Irvine, *AIM Report*, see Judy Doody and Mark Feist, July 1, 2001.

305 Kenneth W. Starr, Independent Counsel, *Report on the Death of Vincent W. Foster*, October 10, 1997, p.64.

306 Kenneth W. Starr, Independent Counsel, *Report on the Death of Vincent W. Foster*, October 10, 1997, p. 57 [161]. "Technician Simonello states: Approximately 13 ft. down slope of the victims feet (west) I observed a pair of prescription glasses laying on the ground."

307 Kenneth W. Starr, Independent Counsel, *Report on the Death of Vincent W. Foster*, October 10, 1997, p. 57 &58. "When found, Mr. Foster's body was located on a steep berm with his head higher than his feet and his feet pointed essentially straight down the berm. Mr. Foster's eyeglasses were recovered by Park Police Technician Simonello approximately 13 feet below Mr. Foster's feet [161]." "Dr. Lee stated ... that the above facts "support the interpretation that Mr. Foster was wearing his eyeglasses at the time the gun was discharged." [165] Lee Report at 493.

308 CW (Confidential Witness), *WABC's John and Paul Alexander Radio Show on The Strange Death of Vince Foster*, July 14, 2001.

309 CW (Confidential Witness), *WABC's John and Paul Alexander Radio Show on The Strange Death of Vince Foster*, July 14, 2001.

310 Reed Irvine, *AIM Report*, Witness Jeanne Slade, July 1, 2001, access online at: http://www.aim.org/aim-report/aim-report-evidence-proving-foster-was-murdered/.

[311] Kenneth W. Starr, Independent Counsel, *Report on the Death of Vincent W. Foster*, October 10, 1997, p.71 [206] .

[312] Robert B. Fiske Jr., Special Prosecutor, *Fiske Report*, June 30, 1994, p.34.

Also see; Kenneth W. Starr, Independent Counsel, *Report on the Death of Vincent W. Foster*, October 10, 1997, p. 30, USPP Report (Morrissette), Dr. Beyer autopsy.

[313] Robert B. Fiske, Jr., Special Prosecutor, *Report of the Independent Counsel in Re: Vincent Foster, Jr.,* June 30, 1994, Hearings, Volume, 14, 4212, 4213, p. 101.

[314] Christopher Ruddy, "Make-up Artist Links Clinton to Possible Cover-up," *Pittsburgh Tribune-Review,* February 14, 1996, p. 104.

[315] Bill Clinton, *White House Press Briefing,* July 21, 1993, 12:50 pm.

[316] *Final Report of Senate Whitewater Investigation,* June 13, 1996, p.22; access online at: http://www.washingtonpost.com/wp-srv/politics/special/whitewater/committee.pdf.

[317] William Safire, "Essay; Vincent Foster's "Can of Worms," *New York Times,* July 24, 1995; access online at: http://www.nytimes.com/1995/07/24/opinion/essay-vincent-foster-s-can-of-worms.html

[318] Kenneth W. Starr, *Report on the Death of Vincent W. Foster,* October 10, 1997, p. 114.

[319] Linda Tripp, *Starr Report Part III,* p. 4276. See: July 28, 1998, p. 47.

[320] Marinka Peschmann, *The Whistleblower: How the Clinton White House Stayed in Power to Reemerge in the Obama White House and the World Stage* (One Rock Ink, 2012), p. 105. "Finding herself with an atrocious decision for any single parent to have to make—provide for her family or face unemployment, Linda took the Pentagon post. "If you're not loyal to them, the Clintons will

construct a means of forcing your loyalty so you can feed your children," Linda said. "Once they've got you, it's impossible to extricate yourself from their clutches." Linda kicked into survival mode. "All I could think about was 'work hard, keep my mouth shut, nothing bad will happen' and try to regain my careerist status."

## Epilogue

[321] Ambrose Evans-Pritchard, *The Secret Life of Bill Clinton: The Unreported Stories*, (Regnery, 1997); access online at: http://terpsboy.com/Articles/JerryParks.html. Also see Linda Tripp testimony on the murder of Jerry Parks, via *Newsmax*, October 8, 1998, access online at: http://archive.newsmax.com/articles/?a=1998/10/8/03541

[322] Mary Dejevsky, "M is for Monica: an A to Zippergate of the affair," *The Independent, UK*, August 4 1998; access online at: http://www.independent.co.uk/arts-entertainment/m-is-for-monica-an-a-to-zippergate-of-the-affair-1169443.html

[323] Helen Kennedy, "Md Prosecutors Drop Tripp Wiretapping Charges," *New York Daily News*, May 25, 2000; access online at: http://articles.nydailynews.com/2000-05-25/news/18140068_1_book-agent-lucianne-goldberg-linda-tripp-stephen-montanarelli

[324] Defense Department Settles with Linda Tripp," *Associated Press*, November 3, 2003; access online at: http://www.usatoday.com/news/washington/2003-11-03-tripp-lawsuit_x.htm

[325] Jeff Mason, "Hillary Clinton calls Bosnia sniper story a mistake," *Reuters*, March 25, 2008, access online at: http://www.reuters.com/article/2008/03/26/us-usa-politics-clinton-idUSN2540811420080326. Video available here: http://www.youtube.com/watch?v=8BfNqhV5hg4&NR=1

[326] Jack Shafer, "WikiLeaks, Hillary Clinton, and the Smoking Gun," *Slate*, November 29, 2010.

[327] Letter to Secretary of State Hillary Rodham Clinton, March 29, 2011. "On March 29th, the head of the House Oversight Committee fired off a letter to Secretary of State Hillary Clinton over her agency's refusal to turn over documents and information about the ATF "gunwalking" scandal exposed by *CBS News*. "Given the gravity of this matter, this refusal is simply unacceptable," reads the letter from Rep. Darrell Issa (R-Calif.)."

[328] "Obama refuses to 'meddle' in Iran," BBC, June 19, 2009; access online at: http://news.bbc.co.uk/2/hi/8104362.stm

[329] Ben Feller, "Obama: U.S. will not send ground troops to Libya: President says U.S. allies had no choice but to launch limited military operations against Gadhafi forces," *Associated Press*, March 19, 2011; access online at: http://www.salon.com/2011/03/19/libya_obama_military_inte rvention/

[330] Bradley Klapper, "Arab Winter? Unrest sparks debate on US policy," Associated Press, September 14, 2012, access online at: http://www.startribune.com/printarticle/?id=169805366

[331]"Threats force Egyptian Christians to flee," *ASSIST News Service*, September 30, 2012. "Most Christians living near Egypt's border with Israel are fleeing their homes after Islamist militants made death threats and gunmen attacked a Coptic-owned shop, a priest said on Friday, according to Egyptian website Aswat Masriya."

[332] Eli Lake, "U.S. Consulate in Benghazi Bombed Twice in Run-Up to 9/11 Anniversary," *The Daily Beast*, October 2, 2012; access online at: http://www.thedailybeast.com/articles/2012/10/02/u-s-consulate-in-benghazi-bombed-twice-in-run-up-to-9-11-anniversary.html

[333] Jennifer Griffin, "Exclusive: CIA operators were denied request for help during Benghazi attack sources say," *Fox News*, October 26, 2012, access online at:

http://www.foxnews.com/politics/2012/10/26/cia-operators-
were-denied-request-for-help-during-benghazi-attack-sources-
say/

[334] Joel Gehrke, "House asked Clinton to testify on Benghazi,
but she declines due to scheduling conflict," *Washington
Examiner*, November 10, 2012; access online at:
http://washingtonexaminer.com/house-asked-clinton-to-testify-
on-benghazi-but-she-declines-due-to-scheduling-
conflict/article/2513151. Also see: US Secretary of State Hillary
Clinton poised to visit friends in Adelaide next week, *Herald Sun*,
November 13, 2012; access online at:
http://www.heraldsun.com.au/news/national/exclusive-us-
secretary-of-state-hillary-clinton-poised-to-visit-friends-in-
adelaide-next-week/story-fndo471r-1226512913666

[335] Chris Matthews, "President of the World: The Bill Clinton
Phenomenon," *MSNBC*, updated February 11, 2011, access
online at:
http://www.msnbc.msn.com/id/41516424/ns/msnbc_tv-
hardball_with_chris_matthews/. "There isn't a single political
figure today with the global reach and influence of Bill
Clinton—a former U.S. president turned humanitarian and
diplomat extraordinaire. This Presidents' Day, *MSNBC*'s Chris
Matthews will take viewers behind the scenes of Clinton's life in
the one-hour documentary "President of the World: The Bill
Clinton Phenomenon."

[336] Michael Falcone, "Clinton Names Donors to Global
Initiative Meeting, *New York Times*, December 9, 2008; access
online at:
http://thecaucus.blogs.nytimes.com/2008/12/09/clinton-
names-donors-to-global-initiative/

[337] "The Long Demise of Glass-Steagall" Timeline, *PBS;* access
online at:
http://www.pbs.org/wgbh/pages/frontline/shows/wallstreet/
weill/demise.html

338 Tom Cohen, "Clinton says Obama offers a better path forward for America," *CNN*, September 6, 2012; access online at: http://www.cnn.com/2012/09/05/politics/democratic-convention-wrap/index.html

339 Josh Margolin, "Jon-Bubba Twist: MFGlobal hired Clinton's group," *New York Post*, December 6, 2011; access online at: http://www.nypost.com/p/news/national/jon_bubba_twist_2u QpRRaeEVM7RNVGelCojO Also see: Neil W. McCabe, "Claim: Clinton Collected $50K Per Week from MF Global," *Human Events*, December 5, 2011; access online at: http://www.humanevents.com/2011/12/05/claim-clinton-collected-50k-per-month-from-mf-global/. Also see: Azam Ahmed and Ben Protess, "No Criminal Case is Likely in Loss at MF Global, *New York Times*, August 15, 2012; access online at: http://dealbook.nytimes.com/2012/08/15/no-criminal-case-is-likely-in-loss-at-mf-global/

CPSIA information can be obtained at www.ICGtesting.com
Printed in the USA
LVOW07s0157310314

379611LV00001B/23/P